sew!

D0293634

Cath Kidston

sew!

Cath Kidston

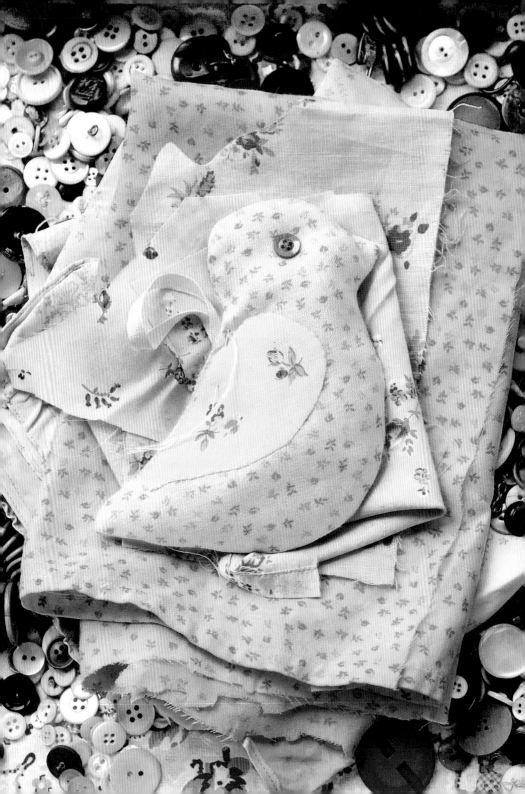

sew!

Cath Kidston

PHOTOGRAPHY BY PIA TRYDE

Quadrille
PUBLISHING

UNLESS OTHERWISE STATED, THE COPYRIGHT AND OTHER INTELLECTUAL PROPERTY RIGHTS
IN ALL DESIGNS AND PATTERNS IN THIS BOOK ARE OWNED BY CATH KIDSTON LIMITED.
FOR THE PURPOSES OF THIS LEGAL NOTICE, ANY USE OF THE DESIGNS OTHER THAN FOR
YOUR OWN PERSONAL USE, INCLUDING RESALE, IS PROHIBITED.

Introduction

I'm amazed at how many of my friends – of all generations – are now taking up needlework, whether they are sewing on a button, shortening the hems of their jeans or making their own cushion covers. Suddenly, sewing seems to be everywhere!

I was taught how to hand sew as a small child. I embroidered coasters and spectacle cases, which were proudly given away as presents, and I can clearly remember learning how to do blanket stitch. As a teenager I progressed to lessons on the school sewing machine and although it took a whole term to make a towelling dressing gown, my enthusiasm remained undiminished. But many of us don't have the first idea how to set about the rewarding process of creating something from scratch.

The idea for this book came about because I really felt that there was a gap in the market for a collection of inspiring and interesting sewing projects that would include something to suit everybody, whatever their previous experience. If you're an absolute beginner, an experienced stitcher or someone keen to renew rusty skills, **Sew!** will show you just how to make things yourself – with all the sense of achievement that brings.

If you are like me, you probably don't want to wade through a serious instruction manual but are looking for some practical and clear advice which you'll find in the Sew! Basics section. I also hope to encourage and inspire you at the same time. There are over forty projects in this book which range from old standbys like the covered coat hangers, that can be made in an hour or so, to more long-term undertakings like

the charming patchwork cot quilt. I hope you'll find something that appeals amongst the various napkins, lavender pillows, aprons, cushions and the many different bags, which include a cool iPod holder, a traditional duffel and my favourite new idea, the quirky inside-out tote.

Some of the best fun I had when planning the book was going through my textile archive, choosing precisely which prints and colourways to use for each project. As well as my own designs, there are old and new florals, stripes, ginghams, vintage linen and soft cotton sheeting. You'll see some of my tips on fabric choices as you read through the pages: mix and match patterns, go for detailed embellishments in clashing colours and always try out unexpected combinations. These are your starting points and you can develop and customise the basic designs as you wish. It's up to you how far you want to go and the journey is so rewarding.

All of the paper patterns are included, so there is no excuse not to start straightaway! Before long, you'll find you have a sewing project permanently on the go. I've always found getting started is easy: the hard bit is putting it down!

Cath Kidston

Sew! Basics

Essential Equipment

All the fabric and haberdashery needed for each project is detailed in the 'what you will need' lists. One of the last items is always 'sewing kit' – the basic tools required for all your needlework. You may already have many of them, but here's my guide to sewing box essentials.

NEEDLES

There are several types of needle, each designed for a particular task. They come in different lengths and diameters, from a thick '1' to a fine '10' for the most delicate work. Start off with a mixed packet, which will include:

• medium-length 'sharps' with small eyes for thread. These are for general stitching and tacking.

• 'crewel' needles which have longer eyes to accommodate thicker embroidery cotton. These are easier to thread and fine for hand-sewing too.

• short 'quilting' needles go easily through layers of fabric and wadding with a stabbing action.

• a large, blunt tapestry needle or larger bodkin will be useful for threading cords or elastic.

PINS

I always use long, slender glass-headed pins, which are not only pretty, but easy to spot against patterned fabric. Keep them in a pincushion or tin, with a magnet close to hand in case they spill.

SEWING THREADS

No. 50 mercerized sewing cotton is an all-purpose thread for stitching on natural fibres, so it's good for these projects. Match thread to the main shade of your fabric; if this isn't possible, go a shade darker. Use a contrasting colour for tacking so you can easily unpick stitches. Use strong buttonhole

thread for securing upholstered buttons, like those on the floor cushions. If you are doing a lot of hand quilting, use special quilter's thread.

THIMBLE

Using a thimble can feel awkward, but persevere if you want to avoid punctured fingertips! They come in various sizes, so choose one that fits snugly but not too tightly on your middle finger.

SCISSORS

You will need three basic pairs in three sizes:

• small embroidery scissors with narrow, pointed blades. Use these for snipping buttonholes, trimming threads and clipping curves and corners.

• a pair of medium-sized general purpose scissors for cutting out smaller items and your paper patterns.

• bent-handled dressmaker's shears for accurate fabric cutting. Invest in a good pair with steel blades and don't ever, ever use them for paper!

• pinking shears are also useful, but not essential. They produce a decorative zigzagged edge that reduces fraying on un-neatened seams.

MEASURING UP

A good tape measure is invaluable. Look for a non-stretchy plastic one with metal tips. A clear ruler, marked with cm divisions is useful when marking quilting lines, seams or buttonhole positions.

MARKING TOOLS

Use water-soluble or fading ink pens to transfer markings onto fabric, or traditional tailor's chalk or chalk pencils are just as good. Use a light colour on dark fabrics and vice versa. A sharp HB pencil will give a fine, accurate line to guide your quilting.

top tip

MORE USEFUL ITEMS WITH WHICH TO STOCK YOUR WORK BASKET INCLUDE: A NEEDLE-THREADER, A SEAM UNPICKER, A BIG REEL OF WHITE SEWING THREAD, SOME SPARE MACHINE NEEDLES, A CARD OF ELASTIC AND A TIN FOR SPARE BUTTONS, BUCKLES, SAFETY PINS AND OTHER ACCUMULATED BITS AND BOBS.

Sewing Machines

The range of sewing machines that is now on the market can seem a bit bewildering, whether you're a new enthusiast or an old hand who has been stitching for years! There is a huge choice available, from entry-level machines which have no extra gadgets, to highly technical electronic versions with pre-programmed stitches, alphabets and LCDs, that can be linked up to your own computer to create complex embroidery designs.

They may look different, but all have the same basic functions and all you need to make up any of my projects is a solid, functional machine that will give you a regular straight stitch with an even tension.

HOW THEY WORK

All sewing machines work by linking two threads, one above the fabric and one below it, to produce a lock stitch. The upper reel is threaded through the arm of the machine, and down to the needle whilst the lower thread is wound onto a small bobbin. For a straight stitch the needle stays in one central position, but for buttonholes and zigzags it moves from side to side. Original hand machines do not have this swing-needle function, but many are still in working order.

THE PARTS OF THE MACHINE

Take time to read through the manual that comes with your machine. This will have a useful diagram that labels all the various dials and switches: study this carefully and get familiar with the terminology. However complicated the computerised element may be, all machines have the same working parts and structure.

• The **spool pin** sits at the top right of the machine. Slip your reel of sewing cotton onto this and follow the manual's instructions to thread the end through to the needle.

• The **bobbin winder** is also on the top of the machine. This is used for winding thread from the main reel onto the small bobbins that carry the lower thread.

• The **tension adjuster** alters the amount of pressure on the upper thread.

• The **needle** screws into the arm of the machine, just in front of the presser foot. It has a hole at the tip, unlike a sewing needle. There are various sizes: you need a 'universal' or medium size 14/90 for these projects. Remember that the tip must always be sharp, so change needles regularly.

• The **presser foot** maintains pressure on the fabric as it passes under the needle. It lifts up and down with a lever. Machines come with several different feet, with more available for specialised stitching. Apart from the basic foot, you need a zip foot to sew close to piping cord or the teeth of a zip. Other feet are used for hemming, gathering or applying ready-made bias binding.

• The flat **throat plate** has a small hole through which the needle passes to pick up the lower thread. It is marked with a series of parallel lines. Align the edges of your fabric to these as you sew, for a regular seam allowance.

• The **feed dog** is a series of serrated ridges under the throat plate which move up and down to ease the fabric along, as it passes under the presser foot.

• The **bobbin case** is the one working part of the machine that you can't see immediately. It sits under the main bed and houses the bobbin with the lower thread. You can change the tension when necessary by adjusting the small grub screw.

• The **reverse stitch control** is very useful as it enables you to work a few stitches in the opposite direction at the beginning and end of each seam to prevent unravelling.

• The **foot pedal** plugs into the machine and is your speed control. Like a car's accelerator, the harder you press, the faster the machine will go.

TENSION

A line of machine stitching should look the same on both sides. Do a sample row before starting work and if you can see a row of loops on one side, there is a problem with the tension. Check your manual and adjust the top or bottom thread.

top tip → ALWAYS USE THE SAME THREAD AT THE TOP AND BOTTOM OF THE MACHINE. IT'S A GOOD IDEA TO BUY SOME EXTRA BOBBINS AND FILL THEM BEFORE YOU START ON A NEW PROJECT – THIS WAY YOU CAN CHANGE OVER QUICKLY WHEN THE THREAD RUNS OUT.

Making
The Patterns

THE PATTERN SHEET

Tucked into the pocket is a large, cleverly designed pattern sheet, which is printed on both sides with a series of coloured geometric shapes. At first glance this might seem to be a rather complicated underground map or circuit diagram. Look closely and you'll see that each individual outline represents a clearly distinguishable pattern piece, which is marked with a letter from A through to Z and all the way up to PP.

Here are all the patterns that you will need to make the projects. Some of these shapes are one-offs – you'll easily spot 'W', the pattern for the quilted hottie cover and 'T', which is the specs case. Others are multipurpose and are used in two or more projects – for instance, the largest circle 'Y' is the pattern for the top and bottom of the beanie cushion but it also doubles up as a bath hat.

MAKING YOUR OWN PATTERNS

All of the outlines are actual size and include the seam allowance, so you can trace them off directly to make your own paper patterns. The quickest way to do this is to spread out the sheet and fix a length of ordinary greaseproof paper over your chosen shape, using lo-tack tape. Draw around the outside edge with a sharp pencil, using a ruler to help keep the lines straight if necessary.

Alternatively you can buy a pack of dressmaker's squared paper, which is marked with the same 1cm grid as the pattern sheet, and simply copy the pattern pieces onto this, transferring the measurements exactly.

PATTERN MARKINGS

As well as the letters, some of the pieces have an extra broken line drawn across them, which

represents an alternative cutting line. The main shape of the oven glove, for instance, is 'U', and line '1u' marks the size of the mitts at each end.

Some of the squares and rectangles have additional broken inner lines, which will give you rounded corners. The instructions will always tell you when to follow these lines.

Other pattern shapes have one side indicated with a dotted line with a double-headed bent arrow pointing towards it. This indicates that the side of the pattern should be placed along folded fabric, to give you a double width or length.

CUTTING OUT GUIDES

Each of the projects has its own cutting out guide. Like the diagram on a dressmaking pattern, this shows you just which pattern pieces you will need and how best to lay them out on your fabric. The fabric quantities in the 'what you will need' shopping list always allow an extra 5cm all round from the minimum amount required, but if you want to match up prints or stripes you will need to buy extra fabric. These guides are shown on a grid, so that you can use them to scale up the shapes if the pattern sheet ever goes astray.

FABRIC GRAIN

You'll see that some of the pattern pieces on the cutting out guides are marked with a double-headed arrow, pointing from top to bottom of the page. This indicates the direction of the straight, lengthwise grain of the fabric, which runs parallel to the sides or selvedges. The cross grain – the bias – runs diagonally across the fabric and has a certain amount of 'give'. Some of the pieces, such as binding strips, have to be cut on the bias so that they will stretch.

top tip

TRANSFER ALL THE MARKINGS, INCLUDING THE LETTERS, TO YOUR PATTERN PIECES BEFORE YOU CUT THEM OUT. KEEP THE PIECES FOR EACH PROJECT TOGETHER IN LARGE LABELLED ENVELOPES SO THAT YOU WILL BE ABLE TO REUSE THEM AT A FUTURE DATE.

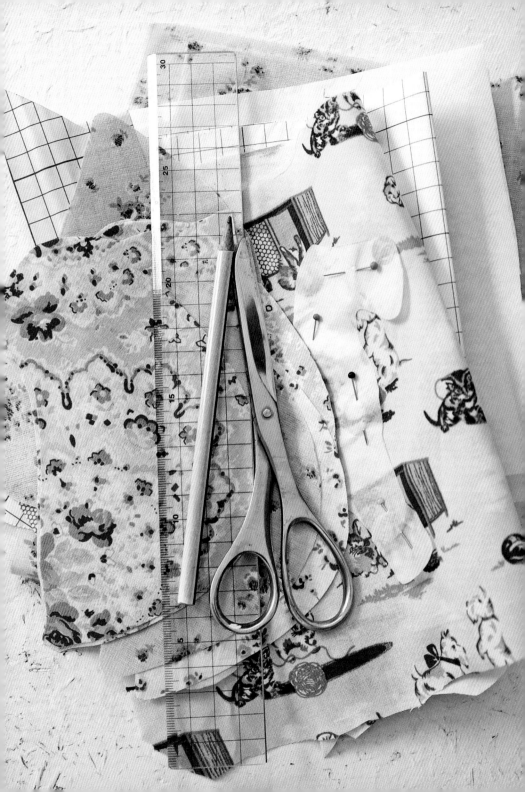

Hems & Edges

A raw edge can be neatened in two ways: either by turning it back and stitching it down to make a hem, or by binding it with a narrow strip of fabric.

A single hem, with just one turning, is used for dressmaking and soft furnishings. Most of the projects require a double hem, which has two turnings. This gives a firmer edge, which is often top-stitched. The depth of the turnings will always be given in the step-by-step instructions.

A bound hem gives a very professional finish, especially if you use a contrasting fabric. You can buy bias binding – a narrow pre-folded strip of plain cotton – in a range of colours and two widths, or make your own from a co-ordinating print.

SINGLE HEM
Firstly, zigzag the edge of the fabric. With the wrong side facing, fold the edge up to the given measurement. You can use a ruler to make sure the hem is a consistent depth. Pin the turning, then tack it if you wish, and machine stitch, just below the neatened edge.

DOUBLE HEM
Fold and press the first turning to the required depth, then make the second turning, as directed. The first turning is usually shorter, but sometimes they are both equal. Pin and tack in place, then either machine stitch close to the inner fold or slip stitch by hand. Top stitch the outer fold on a pocket.

BOUND STRAIGHT EDGES
Open out one edge of the binding and, with right sides facing, pin it to the edge of the fabric. Machine stitch along the first fold. Turn the binding over to the wrong side and tack it down close to the fold. Finish by slip stitch as for the curved corner, or machine stitch on the right side, just inside the edge of the binding.

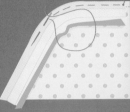

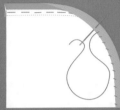

BOUND CURVES

A bound curve on a single layer of fabric needs to be reinforced with stay-stitch – a row of machine stitching worked about 4mm from the edge – to prevent it curling inwards. With right sides facing, tack the edge of the binding along the curve. Gather it in slightly so that the centre fold will fit comfortably around the outside edge without pulling.

Fold the rest of the binding to the back and sew down the edge by hand or machine. You may find that it helps to steam press the curve along the folded edge of the binding before you stitch.

MAKING YOUR OWN BINDING

For a straight edge, you can cut the fabric strips along the grain of the fabric, but for a curved edge they should be on the bias. Trim the ends diagonally, at 45 degrees. To join two strips, pin together with the right sides facing and the ends overlapping as shown. Seam between the points where they cross.

Press the seams open and trim off the projecting triangles. Fold the strip in half lengthways, with wrong sides together and press. Press each edge in turn towards the centre fold.

Seams

Joining two pieces of fabric is the most basic of all sewing techniques, and if you can do it neatly and accurately, you're ready to create any of the projects in this book!

Careful preparation pays off, and if you are new to sewing, it's worth tacking your seams together once they are pinned. This temporary stitch holds the fabric in place as you machine stitch, and is more stable than pins alone. Use a contrasting thread and sew with long running stitches, just inside the seam line.

When you're making an item that will be laundered or that will undergo heavy wear, it's a good idea to neaten the edges with a zigzag or binding, either before you join the seam or afterwards.

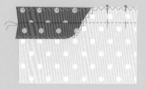

STRAIGHT SEAM
Pin the two pieces together with right sides facing and the edges aligned. Stitch along the given seam allowance, using the footplate lines as a width guide. Reinforce each end with a few extra stitches and press the allowance open or to one side, as directed.

CORNER SEAM
When you reach a corner, keep the needle down and lift the presser foot. Turn the fabric and continue along the next edge. Trim the allowance, to within 2mm of the stitch line. Turn right side out and gently ease the corner into shape with a blunt pencil.

T-JUNCTION SEAM
This seam is used to give width to bags. Join the side and bottom seams and press open. Refold the open corner so that the ends of the seams are aligned. Pin the two sides together and stitch. Trim the allowance and bind or zigzag to neaten.

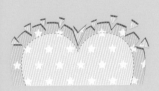

CURVED SEAMS

Trim the allowance back to 6mm so that the seam will not be too bulky. For outside curves, like the top of a heart, cut out a series of regularly spaced little notches to within 2mm of the stitch line. For inside curves, make a series of snips at right angles to the stitching.

CLOSING A GAP

Sometimes you'll need to leave a gap in a seam through which to add the filling. Press back the seam allowance on each side before turning right side out. Pin the two edges together and slip stitch, passing the needle through the edges of the folds for an unobtrusive finish.

TOP STITCHING

Use this to secure folded edges or to reinforce a seam. On a fold, stitch 3mm in from the edge using the presser foot opening as a guide. For a straight or curved seam, press the allowance to one side, then stitch through all three layers from the right side, 3mm from the join.

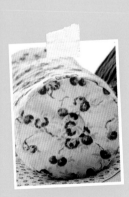

CIRCULAR SEAM

Cut 6mm notches around the circle and 1cm slits at the end of the fabric tube, spaced 2cm apart. Fold the circle and tube four times to give eight equal divisions. Mark the ends of the folds. Pin together, right sides facing, matching marks. Tack just inside the seam line, then machine with the circle on top.

PIPED SEAM

Piping – fabric-covered cord sewn between the two layers – defines a seam visually. Cut a narrow bias strip and fold it around a length of cord with wrong sides facing. Tack close to the cord and unpick any visible tacking once the seam is completed.

Fastenings

A visit to your local haberdashers or needlework supplier will show you just how many different types of fastenings exist. Some of these you may have already used when making clothes or soft furnishings: press-studs, hooks and eyes, fabric-covered buttons and zips, whilst others are designed specifically for homeware and accessories, such as magnetic bag fasteners and spring toggles.

I always love to add extra detail by using traditional hand-sewing techniques, and the buttonhole stitch loops used on the specs case and quilted purse are my current favourites. I used tailored rouleau loops for the hottie and shoulder bag. Handmade buttonholes, also worked in tailor's buttonhole stitch, give individual character to the shoulder bag strap and the large tote – and the effort and patience involved in creating them will pay off in the end!

  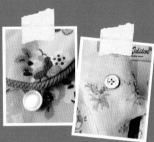

BUTTONS
Although I've used them to fasten most of the bags and cases in this book, buttons have many other decorative purposes. Fabric-covered buttons are ideal for upholstering cushions, and I've used shirt buttons as the finishing touch on the lavender pillow, and as eyes for the various appliqué birds and the Stanley toy. Scour antique and charity shops for one-off examples, salvage them from old garments and sort through the family button tin to find vintage examples in pressed glass, painted plastic, metal, wood or lustrous mother-of-pearl.

HANDMADE BUTTONHOLE
Draw a line, the same size as your button, along the grain of the fabric. Reinforce it with two lines of back stitches. Carefully cut along the line. Using a long length of stranded cotton, sew a round of tailor's buttonhole stitch around the slit, curving each end. Stitch from right to left, inserting the needle upwards, then pulling it back towards you so that the looped thread forms a small knot at the base of each stitch.

BUTTONHOLE STITCH LOOP

This is also worked in stranded thread. Fasten on at the edge of the fabric and make a foundation bar of three or four loose stitches. Starting from the right, work tailor's buttonhole stitch over the threads, looping the thread twice under the needle as shown. Fasten off at the left.

ROULEAU LOOP

A rouleau is a narrow flexible tube, made from a bias strip of fabric. Fold the strip in half and stitch about 3mm from the fold, slanting the end of the seam out to the corner. Trim back the seam allowance to 3mm. Thread a tapestry needle with strong thread, fasten it to the corner and tie the ends together. Pass the needle carefully through the tube so that the fabric is gradually turned right side out.

ZIPS

This is a quick method for inserting a zip into a seam. Press back a 2cm turning along each edge, then tack the two folds loosely together. Tack the closed zip securely to the wrong side, so that the teeth lie exactly along the join. Fit a zip foot and sew the zip in place 6mm from the outside edge of the teeth. Stitch three times across the top and bottom edges at right angles. Unpick the tacking.

Ties & Handles

Ties and handles can be viewed as purely functional aspects of a design – the means by which you carry a bag, for example – but in fact they provide a great opportunity to add extra detailing, such as a splash of contrasting colour or a new texture.

You can buy some interesting ready-made handles, like the cane loops bound with scarlet twine that I hunted down for the knitting bag, but you can easily make your own from folded and stitched strips of fabric. A similar construction technique is used for apron ties and these are particularly effective when a plain colour is used alongside a print: take a look at the cowboy apron on page 94.

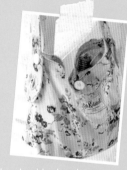

TWO-PART HANDLE
The button-on strap for the shoulder bag has rounded ends, and so I made it from two pieces of fabric. These were sewn together with a gap left in the seam, then turned right side out and top stitched. A similar strap with square ends could be made by the folded handle method opposite, which is more straightforward.

REINFORCING STITCHING
Give additional strength to the ends of your handle with reinforcing stitching. Machine stitch a square or rectangle, then sew diagonal lines between the corners.

WEBBING
Webbing is a sturdy woven tape, which you can find in subtle natural cotton colours or more vivid nylon shades. It comes in widths from around 2cm to 8cm. I used a 4cm webbing to make the handle on the shopper bag, stitching the two edges together along the centre, so it is easier to grip.

FOLDED HANDLE OR TIE

Press the strip in half lengthways with right sides facing, then press the sides to the centre. Tack, then top stitch the two edges to make a strong, open-ended strap. You can sew the ends together to make a looped handle. To mitre the ends, fold and press each corner inwards at 45 degrees before pressing in the sides. Press the end triangles inwards.

NARROW TIES

The washbag's stylish ties are made from long rouleaux. Dressmakers use a thin latchet hook to turn these through, but you can use the method on page 25. Pull the needle slowly, so the fabric doesn't get jammed. The jewellery roll ties are a cheat's way of making a similar fabric tie: simply slip stitch together the folded edges of a length of bias binding.

CORD

I chose a soft woven cotton cord for the duffel bag. Piping cord, which would work equally well, is twisted and a little firmer. It comes in various thicknesses from around 4mm–12mm. The iPod case has a drawstring made from the narrow nylon cord used for Roman blinds. You'll find both this and piping cord at furnishing suppliers.

Appliqué & Quilting

Appliqué – creating designs from cut-out fabric shapes – is a great way to use up all kinds of scraps and offcuts. I like to work with Bondaweb, the quickest way to trace and fix down the motifs, but tried out a more traditional technique for the Bird Cushion. The full-size trace-off templates are tucked into the pocket. Remember that you may need to reverse these outlines, as iron-on appliqué always gives you a mirror image of the original template.

IRON-ON APPLIQUÈ

Read the manufacturer's instructions before starting work, and check the heat setting on your iron. Use a pressing cloth if you are working with felt.

1 Trace the outlines onto the paper side of the Bondaweb with a pencil. Cut them out roughly, leaving a small margin around each shape.

2 Place the motifs onto the wrong side of the fabric, with the paper upwards, fitting them together like a jigsaw. Press down with a dry iron.

3 Cut each shape out around the outline. Peel off the papers and position them on the background fabric, adhesive downwards. Press in place.

EDGING THE MOTIFS

Edging each element with a round of stitching is both practical and decorative: it prevents any fraying and adds extra definition to the shapes.

STRAIGHT STITCH

You can finish each motif by hand with small straight stitches worked at right angles to the edge in sewing cotton or stranded embroidery thread.

ZIGZAG

An open zigzag, machined in plain white, gives a hardwearing finish to items that will need to be laundered.

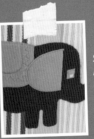

SATIN STITCH

A narrow satin stitch edging is the most functional of all. Match the sewing thread to the colours of the felt.

TURNED-EDGE APPLIQUÉ

Start off by tracing or photocopying the motif and cut out each separate element from paper. You can use the paper templates several times.

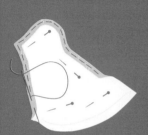

1 Pin the template to your fabric with wrong sides upwards. Cut out leaving a 4mm allowance, then fold this margin over and tack down.

2 Press to set the fold and unpick the papers. Pin the shape in position and slip stitch the folded edge to the background.

3 For a raised effect, gently push a small amount of polyester filling under the shape before stitching it down.

QUILTING

Quilting gives a raised, padded look to fabric and the technique can be as sophisticated as the Quilted Purse on page 136 or as cosy as a padded hottie cover. Simply sandwich a piece of cotton batting or polyester wadding between your main fabric and a backing fabric, and stitch all three layers together.

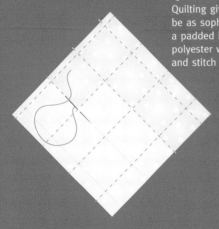

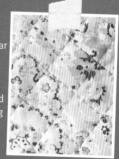

For a diamond pattern, use a clear ruler, a set square and a sharp pencil to mark a grid across the surface of your fabric. Tack the three layers together securely and stitch along the pencil lines using a short quilting needle.

Decorative Details

If you love textiles as much as I do, you are sure to have your own hoard of trimmings, stored away and awaiting a new lease of life. Used with discretion, lace, braid or ricrac can provide the perfect detail that completes a project and adds a personal touch.

A narrow border of crisp white lace will enhance a sprigged floral print, and always looks great with its natural partner, vintage linen. Try an edging of primary coloured ricrac or a ribbon bow to bring out the brighter tones within a fabric design, and if you can't get a precise match, follow my example and go for a gloriously clashing contrast. You can add accents of colour with velvet bows, but sometimes a simple bias binding or cotton tape will work just as well. Good haberdashery departments and specialist stores have an enticing array of new trimmings, and you can easily find vintage lace and ribbons at flea markets, antique dealers and even charity shops if you persevere and if you enjoy a good rummage.

Embroidery is another effective way to add colour and fine detail, such as the cowboy lassos on the boy's apron or Stan's name on his dog tag. Hanks of stranded cotton threads come in a rainbow of colours. Use all six strands and a long-eyed needle for bold stitches, and a few threads and a finer needle for more delicate work.

HAND STITCHES
Most of the projects in the book are sewn by machine, but you'll find that they also involve a few hand and embroidery techniques. Most of these are explained in the step-by-step instructions, but here are a few other basic stitches, which you may find useful.

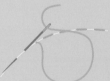

RUNNING STITCH
This is worked on a large scale when you are tacking or gathering, and on a smaller scale for hand quilting. The spaces and the stitches should always be a consistent length.

BACK STITCH
Use this for hand seaming on small projects and for 'writing'. Take the needle backwards and down through the fabric, then bring it back up one stitch length ahead of the first stitch.

CHAIN STITCH
This gives you a broad, flexible line. Loop the thread under the point of the needle from left to right before you pull it through, then take the needle back down through the loop of the last stitch.

RICRAC

There's something very appealing about ricrac braid – it always looks cheerful and comes in wonderful colours. If you set it into a seam or under a turned back hem, you get a little row of scallops peeping out. I used bright red ricrac to trim the rosebud Egg Cosy and a broader, more subtle yellow to edge the flap of the Quilted Purse.

LACE

Border lace has one straight and one curvy edge. Work a row of running stitches along the straight edge and pull up the thread if you want a gathered effect, or leave it flat for a plainer look. The torchon lace I used on the Lavender Pillow was a lucky find from my local sewing shop. For the Bath Hat I used a narrower and more practical broderie anglaise with a pre-gathered edge.

RIBBON

The double-face velvet ribbon used to embellish the Heart Pincushion was a bit of an extravagance, but as I only needed a short length it was worth splashing out for a luxurious finishing touch. However, remember there's more to ribbon than just bows: the Birdie Tablecloth is edged with red and white gingham ribbon that is an exact match for the appliqué fabric.

Sew! Projects

The challenge I set for myself with this book was to design projects that were practical as well as pretty. I selected a variety of items that cover all the basic sewing skills and added in some decorative details. Combing through my fabric archives to find the perfect print for each one was so much fun; the best possible inspiration to pick up a sewing needle and thread!

Square Cushion

what you will need...

• 75 x 65cm striped cotton ticking • 30 x 50cm floral print cotton in similar weight • 2 large buttons • matching sewing thread • sewing kit • sewing machine • 45cm square cushion pad

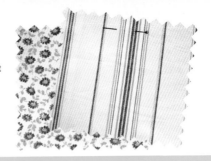

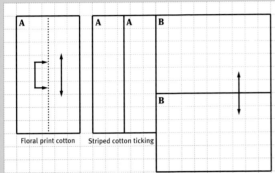

cutting out

Centre front: Cut 1 x A from floral print cotton, on the fold
Side fronts: Cut 2 x A from striped cotton ticking
Back panels: Cut 2 x B from striped cotton ticking

Floral print cotton

Striped cotton ticking

Ticking stripes and pretty floral prints always complement each other, so mix and match the two fabrics to create this deceptively simple cushion. It's an ideal starter project and to make things really easy there's no need to stitch any buttonholes – simply snip off the buttons when the cover needs to be laundered.

The seam allowance throughout is 1.5cm.

1 With right sides facing, sew the side fronts to the long edges of the centre front. Press the seams open.

2 Hem the top edge of the bottom back panel by pressing under 1cm, then a further 4cm. Pin and stitch down. Neaten the lower edge of the top back panel in the same way.

3 Position the cushion front and bottom back panel together, with right sides facing, lining up the raw edges. Lay the top panel in place, again matching the edges.

4 Pin the three pieces together, then sew around all four sides. Clip the corners (see page 22) and turn the cover right side out. Press lightly.

5 Insert the pad and fasten the cover by sewing the buttons securely through both panels, 2cm down from the edge and 12.5cm in from the corners.

top tip

DEPENDING ON THE WIDTH OF THE PATTERN REPEAT, YOU MAY NEED TO ALLOW EXTRA TICKING FABRIC TO ENSURE THAT THE TWO SIDE FRONTS ARE SYMMETRICAL. LINE UP BOTH BACK PANELS CAREFULLY WHEN CUTTING OUT, SO THAT THE STRIPES WILL MATCH ACROSS THE OPENING.

Bolster
Cushion

what you will need...

• 85 x 55cm floral print cotton • 2 x 4cm self-cover buttons • matching sewing thread • buttonhole thread • sewing kit • sewing machine • 50cm bolster cushion pad with 18cm diameter

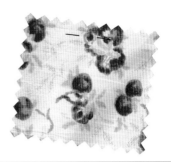

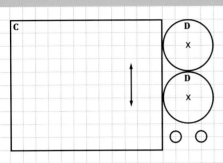

cutting out

Ends: Cut 2 x D. Mark the centre of each circle
Sides: Cut 1 x C
Buttons: Cut 2 circles as specified on kit

There's something about a feather-filled bolster that adds a little boudoir luxury to any setting, and the cylindrical shape makes an impact whether on its own or piled alongside an assortment of other cushions. Don't be put off by the circular seams – you'll find clear instructions for this on page 23.

1 Press back a 1cm turning along each short edge of the main piece.

2 With right sides facing, pin these two edges at the corners. Slip stitch the front and back folds together for 5cm at each end, leaving a long opening between them.

3 Find the centre of each end piece by folding the circles into quarters and mark

this point. Following the diagram and steps on page 23, sew one to each end of the main piece with a 1.5cm seam.

4 Turn the cover right side out and ease the circular seams into shape. Insert the cushion pad through the side opening.

5 Gather up the outside edge of each small circle and slip them over the domed tops of the self-cover buttons. Tighten the threads, then clip on the backings as directed by the manufacturer.

6 Pass a length of buttonhole thread through one of the button shanks and thread both ends through the eye of a large, long needle.

7 Plunge the needle through both the cover and the bolster at the marked centre point, then bring the needle out through the side of the bolster. Pull the thread up tightly and fasten off securely.

8 Pin the edges of the opening together and slip stitch the two folds to complete the cover.

top tip I CHOSE A VINTAGE FRENCH ROSE PRINT FOR MY CUSHION, BUT YOU CAN OPT FOR A MORE FORMAL LOOK BY USING TICKING, CUT SO THE STRIPES RUN EITHER LENGTHWAYS OR AROUND THE COVER. THE TRADITIONAL WAY TO FINISH A BOLSTER IS WITH A CONTRASTING ROUND OF PIPING AT EACH END.

Bird
Cushion

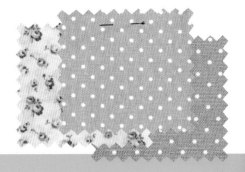

what you will need...

- 50 x 20cm white cotton • 50 x 60cm floral print cotton
- tracing paper and pencil • 15cm square blue spotted fabric
- 15cm square pink spotted fabric • polyester toy filling
- 2 small buttons • 2 black seed beads • green stranded cotton
embroidery thread • 1m 12mm-wide ricrac • matching sewing
thread • sewing kit • sewing machine • 30 x 45cm cushion pad

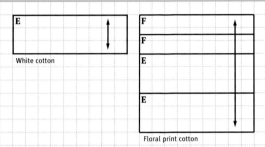

E

White cotton

F
F
E

E

Floral print cotton

cutting out

Centre front: Cut 1 x E from white cotton
Top and bottom front: Cut 2 x F from
   floral print cotton
Back panels: Cut 2 x E from floral print
   cotton

templates

Small bird and Mini bird

You'll find these dear little birds popping up in different guises throughout the book! Here I've used the motif in both sizes to make a whole family in turned-edge appliqué, complete with padded wings. The combination of yellow ricrac, crisp spots and ditsy flowers gives a spring-like freshness to the design.

1 Following the steps on page 29, make up the body and wing pieces for the four birds, reversing two of them. Sew the bodies to the centre front. Add the beads to the small birds and the buttons to the large birds for eyes.

2 Stitch a length of ricrac to the top and bottom of the centre front, so that the curves

just touch the edge of the fabric. Pin the top and bottom fronts in place, with right sides facing.

3 Machine stitch the seams 6mm from the edge. Carefully press so that the ricrac curves point outwards and the seam allowances lie inwards. Embroider the green grass with a few lines of straight stitch.

4 Hem one long edge of each back panel. Place the cushion front right side upwards, then position the back panels along the top and bottom, with raw edges aligned. Pin together and seam all four sides, 1cm from the edge.

5 Clip the corners and turn the cover right side out. Insert the cushion pad and slip stitch the opening to close.

top tip

IF YOU CAN'T FIND THE RIGHT SIZE PAD, YOU CAN QUICKLY MAKE YOUR OWN BESPOKE FILLING FROM TWO RECTANGLES OF CALICO CUT 2CM LARGER ALL ROUND THAN THE FINISHED COVER. JOIN WITH A 1CM SEAM, TURN THROUGH, AND STUFF WITH POLYESTER WADDING. SLIP STITCH TO CLOSE.

Floor
Cushion

what you will need...

• 140 x 90cm floral print cotton duck • 5 x 2.5cm self-cover buttons • 5 x 2.5cm buttons • buttonhole thread • upholstery needle • matching sewing thread • sewing kit • sewing machine • 50 x 50 x 10cm foam cushion pad

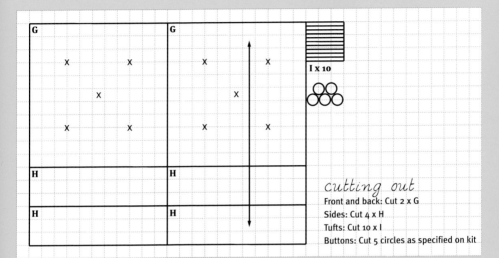

cutting out

Front and back: Cut 2 x G
Sides: Cut 4 x H
Tufts: Cut 10 x I
Buttons: Cut 5 circles as specified on kit

Long summer days are just made for outdoor living and these thick, square cushions will ensure your creature comforts whether you're at a festival, picnicking, camping, or simply lounging about in the garden. You'll need a specially long and strong upholstery needle to secure the buttons that give them their special padded look.

1 Mark the 5 button positions on the front and back pieces, one at the centre and four points 20cm diagonally in from each corner.

2 Pin the long edge of the first side to one edge of the front piece. Starting and finishing the seam 1.5cm in from the raw edges, machine stitch together with a 1.5cm seam. Join the other three sides to the front in the same way.

3 Now pin and stitch the short edges of all four sides together to make a shallow box. Seam each edge from the point where it meets the front to 1.5cm from the corner.

top tip

GETTING THE BUTTONS TO SINK RIGHT BACK INTO THE FOAM FILLING ACTUALLY TAKES QUITE A BIT OF EFFORT, SO BE PREPARED TO WORK HARD! SEE IF YOU CAN RECRUIT A FRIEND TO HELP PUSH THE PAD DOWN ON EITHER SIDE OF THE BUTTON POSITIONS AS YOU PULL THE THREAD.

Floor Cushion

4 Carefully trim a small triangle of fabric from all three pieces at each corner.

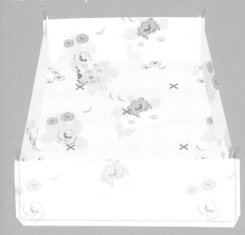

5 Pin and stitch three edges of the front panel to the 'box' in the same way and clip the corners.

6 Turn the cover right side out and press under a 1.5cm turning along the two open edges. Insert the cushion pad and pin the folded edges together. Slip stitch from corner to corner.

7 Cover the buttons as directed. Fold two tuft strips into loops, overlapping the ends by 2cm, then cross one over the other. Thread 50cm of buttonhole thread through a button and pass both ends through the upholstery needle. Plunge the needle into the front of the cushion at a marked point.

8 Push the needle right through the pad, bringing it out at the corresponding mark on the back. Pass the ends of the thread through the holes in a plain button. Pull up tightly so that the buttons sink into the pad. Knot and trim the ends. Add the other buttons in the same way.

top tip

HIGH DENSITY SEATING FOAM CAN BE ORDERED FROM SPECIALIST SUPPLIERS, WHO WILL CUT IT TO THE EXACT SIZE AND DEPTH REQUIRED. ASK FOR A STOCKINETTE WRAP, WHICH SOFTENS THE EDGES, PROTECTS THE FOAM AND MAKES IT EASIER TO GET THE PAD INSIDE YOUR COVER.

Flower Cushion

what you will need...

- 35 x 55cm white cotton • 50 x 80cm red cotton • selection of floral print cotton scraps • bondaweb • pencil • matching sewing threads • sewing kit • sewing machine • 35 x 50cm cushion pad

template
Small flower

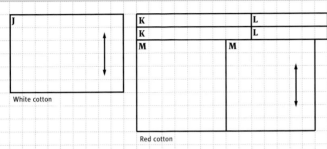

J	K	L	
	K	L	
White cotton	M	M	
	Red cotton		

cutting out

Front: Cut 1 x J from white cotton

Top and bottom borders: Cut 2 x K from red cotton

Side borders: Cut 2 x L from red cotton

Back panels: Cut 2 x M from red cotton, following square corners

Stitchers are magpies at heart and inevitably acquire a ragbag, bulging with remnants, offcuts and fabric salvaged from old garments. In a spirit of 'make do and mend' I chose some favourite vintage prints to appliqué this red, blue and white cushion: a great way to utilise the tiniest scraps.

The seam allowance throughout is 1cm.

1 Decide which two prints to use for each motif. I alternated red and blue flowers so the outlines stood out where they overlap.

2 Following the inner outlines, trace twenty ovals (two lots of six petals, plus eight leaves), two small circles for the centres, two flower heads and four stalks onto Bondaweb. Cut out and iron onto the prints.

3 Iron down each complete motif in turn, starting at the right and working towards the left. Edge each shape with straight stitch.

4 Trim 6cm from one short edge of J, so it measures 39cm.

5 Stitch a side border to each side edge of the front and press the seams outwards. Add the top and bottom borders, again pressing the seams outwards.

6 Make a 1cm double hem along one side edge of each back panel. Lay the completed front with the right side facing upwards and place one panel, right side down, across each side, so hems overlap in the centre.

7 Pin the three pieces together and machine stitch around all four sides. Clip the corners, turn right side out and press.

8 Insert the pad through the opening. Instead of buying a pad, you can make one from two 37 x 52cm rectangles of calico: see the 'top tip' for the Bird Cushion on page 40.

top tip

TO MAKE SURE THAT THE MOTIFS ARE EVENLY SPACED, LAY ALL THE PIECES OUT ON THE CUSHION FRONT BEFORE YOU REMOVE THE BACKING PAPERS AND MARK THEIR POSITIONS WITH A FADING PEN. ALLOW A 2CM BORDER AT THE SIDES AND 4CM ALONG THE TOP AND BOTTOM EDGES.

Padded
Placemats

what you will need...

• 35 x 85cm laundered plaid cotton duck • 30 x 40cm pre-shrunk cotton batting
• matching sewing thread • sewing kit • fading pen • ruler • sewing machine

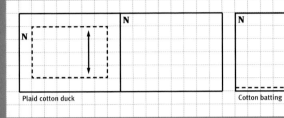

Plaid cotton duck

Cotton batting

cutting out

Front and Back: Cut 2 x N from
plaid cotton duck
Padding: Cut 1 x N from cotton
batting. Trim 12mm from
one long and one short side

Placemats are on the list of useful items that everybody needs at some time, whether it's to protect a polished wooden surface or to add colour to a table setting. Make your own from fabric that co-ordinates with your cutlery, crockery and glassware, and you'll find that every mealtime takes on a festive air.

1 Use a fading pen and a ruler to mark a rectangle, 5cm in from the edge, on the right side of the front panel. Pin the padding the wrong side of this panel, centring it so that there is a 5mm margin all round. Tack it in place.

2 Now pin the back panel to the front panel with right sides facing, so that the front panel is sandwiched between the padding and the back.

3 Machine stitch the three layers of fabric and padding together, leaving a 20cm gap along the centre of the bottom edge. Sew 5mm from the edge, so that the stitches run just outside the edge of the padding.

4 Press back the seam allowance along each side of the opening, clip the corners and turn the placemat right sides out through the gap (see page 22). Tack the opening, making sure the seam allowances lie flat, and slip stitch to close.

5 Machine stitch along the marked line on the front using thread to match or contrast with the main fabric. Finish off with a round of top stitch, 3mm from the outside edge.

top →
tip

IF YOU USE A PLAID OR CHECK DESIGN AS I DID, SIMPLY FOLLOW THE GEOMETRIC GRID PATTERN TO CUT OUT YOUR MATS AND AS A GUIDE FOR THE RECTANGULAR STITCHING. REMEMBER TO ALLOW EXTRA FABRIC IF YOU WISH TO CENTRE THE PATTERN OR IF YOU ARE GOING TO MAKE A MATCHING SET.

Floral Napkins

what you will need...

• 45cm square floral print cotton duck • 60 x 30cm toning plaid or check cotton duck • matching sewing thread
• sewing kit • sewing machine

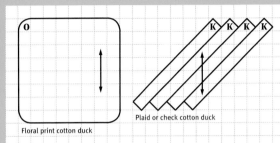

cutting out

Napkin: Cut 1 x O from floral print cotton duck, following the rounded corners

Binding: Cut 4 x K from plaid or check cotton duck, on the bias

The final touch for your table setting has to be a set of napkins. Here I've picked the painterly 'Rose' print on a powder blue background and bordered it with 'Woven Check', the plaid design used for the mats, to show how two mismatched fabrics can look stunning together if they share a colour scheme.

1 Join the four bias strips at the short ends, overlapping the points as shown on page 21. Press the seams open and trim the points in line with the straight edges. Trim the ends at right angles.

2 Press the binding in half widthways, along the entire length, then press under a 5mm turning at one long edge.

3 Stay stitch the corners of the napkin.

4 Starting in the centre of one side, pin and tack the unpressed binding edge around the napkin, right sides facing. Ease the binding around the corners as on page 21.

5 Trim the end of the binding at a right angle when you have completed the round, allowing a 2cm overlap. Press under 5mm at the loose end and tack in place.

6 Turn the other edge of the binding back to the wrong side of the napkin, so that the raw edge is enclosed, and tack down the fold. Finish off by slip stitching the fold in place.

top
tip

OLD-FASHIONED ETIQUETTE DEMANDED NAPKINS IN A RANGE OF SIZES, FROM DAINTY 30CM SQUARES FOR AFTERNOON TEA UP TO ENORMOUS STARCHED DAMASK VERSIONS FOR FORMAL DINNERS. MAKE YOURS IN THE SIZE THAT SUITS YOU BEST, ENLARGING THE 45CM SQUARE IF NECESSARY.

Heart
Teatowel

what you will need...

- 65 x 80cm white linen • 25 x 65cm floral print dressweight cotton
- 20cm squares of 6 floral prints • bondaweb • matching sewing thread • sewing kit • sewing machine

template
Large heart

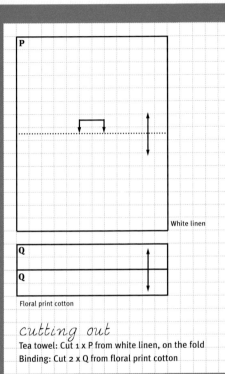

White linen

Q

Q

Floral print cotton

cutting out
Tea towel: Cut 1 x P from white linen, on the fold
Binding: Cut 2 x Q from floral print cotton

Ditsy floral fabrics always muddle along, side by side, if you keep the patterns on the same scale. I cut six large hearts, each from a different print, to create the iron-on appliqué borders for this teatowel, and edged each one with a round of machine zigzag so that they'll stand up to the daily drying routine.

1 Pin one binding strip, right side down, to each short side of the linen. Machine stitch, 1cm from the edge and press the seam allowances outwards.

2 Press and pin a 1cm double hem along each long side. Top stitch, 3mm from the inside fold.

3 Press under 1cm along the raw edge of both bindings. Turn this to the wrong side and press so that the folds lie just beyond the stitch line. Pin and top stitch from the right side. Slip stitch the open side edges.

4 Trace six hearts onto Bondaweb. Following the technique on page 28, iron each one onto a different fabric. Cut them out and peel off the backing papers.

5 Fold the teatowel in half widthways to find the centre. Position one heart centrally at each end, with the points 1cm away from the binding strips.

6 Iron in place, then add another two hearts at each end, leaving a 2.5cm space on either side of the first motif. Press down. Using white thread, zigzag around each heart by machine.

Following the technique on page 28

top tip → OLD LINEN TABLECLOTHS AND SHEETS HAVE A WONDERFULLY SOFT QUALITY THAT ONLY COMES FROM DECADES OF USE AND LAUNDERING. NOT ALL OF THEM SURVIVE INTACT HOWEVER, SO MAKING ONE-OFF TEATOWELS IS A GOOD WAY TO RECYCLE THE BEST PARTS OF THE FABRIC.

Half
Apron

what you will need...

- 45 x 130cm floral print cotton duck • 2m 2cm-wide bias binding
- matching sewing thread • sewing kit • fading pen • ruler • sewing machine

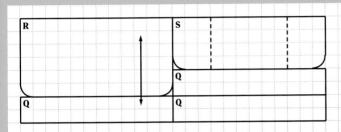

cutting out

Apron: Cut 1 x R
Pocket: Cut 1 x S. Mark a line
15cm from each short side
Ties: Cut 3 x Q

You can brighten up the most mundane household and gardening chores with this practical half apron: its three pockets are just the right size for dusters or secateurs and twine. Select a vivid floral print for maximum cheerfulness and trim the edges with bias binding in an even stronger colour.

1 Following the directions on page 20, neaten the top edge of the pocket with bias binding. Mark the centre point of this edge. Pin the side and bottom edges to the main apron, matching the rounded corners, and machine stitch, leaving a seam allowance of 6mm.

2 To mark the pocket divisions, rule a line 15cm in from each side edge. Sew the two layers together along both lines.

3 Bind the side and bottom edges, referring to the technique for curved corners on page 21.

4 Join the short ends of the three ties to form one long strip and press the seams

open. Press in half lengthways and unfold. Now fold both long edges to the centre crease and press in place. Mitre the short ends following the directions on page 27. Open out the centre fold and fold the strip in half lengthways to find the centre point.

5 Matching up the centre points, pin the apron to the strip so the raw top edge lies along the crease. Pin and tack the top edge of the apron to the lower half of the strip.

6 Turn the upper half of the strip over the top edge of the apron and tack it down. Tack the top and bottom halves of the loose ends together to make the left and right ties. Top stitch 3mm all the way along the short and long edges of the strip.

top tip APRON POCKETS ALWAYS GET THE MOST WEAR AT THE TOP CORNERS, SO WORK A FEW EXTRA REINFORCING STITCHES AT THE TOP END OF THE DIVIDING LINES AND AT THE POINTS WHERE THE TOP CORNERS OF THE POCKET PIECE MEETS THE MAIN APRON.

Egg
Cosy

what you will need...

• 15 x 20cm floral print cotton • 15 x 20cm felt • 20cm ricrac
• matching sewing thread • sewing kit • sewing machine

Floral print cotton   1t   Felt

drawing up the pattern

Cosy: Use piece T with line 1t as the bottom edge
Tab: Use piece I, with line 1i as the right edge

cutting out

Cosy: Cut 2 from floral print cotton
Lining: Cut 2 from felt
Tab: Cut 1 from felt

No breakfast tray is complete without a couple of boiled eggs and plate of 'soldiers'. These jolly cosies are made from a rose print and lined with green felt to keep the eggs toasty warm. The curved seams are machine stitched, but this project is also a good way for practising some basic hand stitching.

1 Fold one cosy piece in half widthways to find the centre line. Fold the tab in half lengthways and tack it centrally along the crease, on the right side, so that the two ends line up with the top edge.

2 Pin the second cosy piece over the first, with right sides facing. Stitch the side and top edges together, with a 5mm seam. Clip a series of notches from the curved part of the seam allowance, spacing them 1cm apart (see page 23).

3 Turn the cosy right side out, ease the seam into position and press lightly.

4 Pin the two felt linings together, and stitch 5mm from the side and top edges. Trim the seam allowance back to 3mm.

5 Slip the lining inside the cosy and line up the open edges. Turn them both up together to make a 5mm hem around the opening. Tack in place.

6 Fold the hem up once again. Starting at the centre back, slip the ricrac behind the turning so that the scallops peep out over the top edge. Trim the ends and tuck them under the hem. Tack through all the layers, then stitch the top edge down.

top tip WHEN YOU ARE CHOOSING TRIMMINGS AND BINDINGS, PICK OUT ONE OR MORE KEY COLOURS FROM THE PRINTED FABRIC. THIS BRIGHT GREEN FELT IS AN EXACT MATCH FOR THE ROSEBUD STEMS AND LEAVES WHILST THE RED RICRAC IS THE SAME COLOUR AS THE DARKEST PETALS.

Birdie
Tablecloth

what you will need...

• plain linen tablecloth or sheet • for each heart and bird repeat:
2 20cm squares gingham cotton, 20 x 25cm floral print cotton,
2 small buttons • bondaweb • matching sewing thread • sewing kit
• gingham ribbon to edge cloth, plus 5cm • sewing machine

templates
Large heart and Large bird

Long refectory tables require extra large tablecloths, which aren't always easy to find, so I created this one-off cover by giving a new lease of life to an antique linen sheet. I added an iron-on appliqué border of large hearts and birds cut from two colours of gingham and a toning floral print. The matching edging, made from gingham ribbon, is a speedy and effective way to finish off the cloth. You could use the small-scale versions of these motifs to embellish a set of napkins to go with the tablecloth.

1 Decide how many repeats of the heart and bird motif you would like. I spaced three at regular intervals along the sides and centred one at each end.

2 You'll find detailed instructions for iron-on appliqué on page 28. For each repeat you will need to trace two birds, two wings and a heart onto Bondaweb. Reverse one of the birds and its wing, so they face each other.

3 Fuse the wings and heart onto the floral print and iron one bird onto each of the ginghams. Varying the fabrics gives extra animation to the finished design, so mix and match the prints and checks for each pair of birds, their wings and the heart. I used three different ginghams in all: red, green and pink.

4 Fold the tablecloth into quarters and press the folds lightly to mark the centre of each side: use this crease as a guideline for ironing down the first motifs. You can then fold the long sides in half again, to mark the positions for the other two repeats.

5 Edge each individual piece, either with a round of short straight stitches or with a machine zigzag or satin stitch. Finish off by stitching the gingham ribbon around the edge of the cloth, mitring it at the corners and overlapping the ends with a neat hem.

top tip

IF YOUR SHEET HAS ANY INDELIBLE MARKS OR HOLES, YOU CAN CONCEAL THEM WITH CAREFULLY POSITIONED MOTIFS. WASH AND IRON THE APPLIQUÉ FABRICS FIRST, AS THE TABLECLOTH IS BOUND TO NEED LAUNDERING AT SOME STAGE AND ANY SHRINKAGE WILL DISTORT THE DESIGN.

Oven
Glove

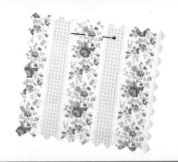

what you will need...

• 35 x 85cm laundered floral print cotton duck • 30 x 40cm pre-shrunk cotton batting • matching sewing thread • sewing kit • fading pen • ruler • sewing machine

drawing up the pattern

Mitts: Use piece U, with line '1u' as the straight edge

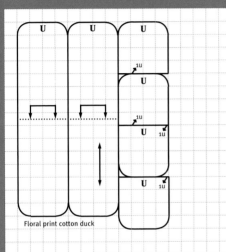

Floral print cotton duck

cutting out

Backing: Cut 2 x U from floral print cotton duck, on the fold
Mitts: Cut 4 from floral print cotton duck
Padding: Cut 1 x U, on the fold, plus 2 x mitts from cotton batting

Here's another re-working of an everyday essential: even if you prefer heating up ready meals to baking wholemeal bread and trays of cupcakes, you'll need to have an oven glove! This project is very easy to put together and makes a good introduction to the techniques involved in binding edges.

1 Start by stacking up the three pieces that make up the first mitt: a mitt with its right side down at the bottom, then a mitt padding in the middle and another mitt on top with its right side upwards.

2 Pin and tack all the layers together around the outside edge. Neaten the straight edge with bias binding, either by hand or machine, as shown in the steps on page 20. Do the same for the second mitt.

3 Sandwich the two backings and the remaining piece of padding together in the same way and tack close to the outside edge.

4 Pin a mitt at each end of the backing and tack in place. Sew a round of bias binding all the way round the outside edge, starting and finishing at the centre of one long edge.

5 Cut a 10cm length from the remaining binding and press under the ends. Fold in half widthways and slip stitch the folds together. Sew the ends securely to the point where the binding meets to make a hanging loop.

top tip

IF YOU'RE WORKING WITH A FABRIC THAT HAS A DIRECTIONAL DESIGN, LIKE THE STRIPES ON THIS 'FLORAL GINGHAM', PLAN THE POSITION OF THE PATTERN PIECES SO THAT THE DESIGN RUNS CENTRALLY ALONG THE BACKING AND MATCHES UP WITH THE MITTS AT EACH END. YOU MAY NEED EXTRA FABRIC FOR THIS.

Peg
Bag

what you will need...

- 40 x 75cm strawberry print cotton duck • child's-size 30cm coat hanger
- 1.5m bias binding • matching sewing thread • sewing kit • sewing machine

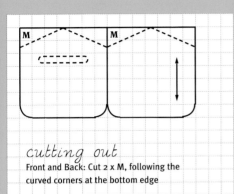

cutting out

Front and Back: Cut 2 x M, following the curved corners at the bottom edge

Hanging out the washing is so much easier when your pegs are close to hand, as our grandmothers knew well. Here's another practical exercise in using bias binding: this time you can learn how to neaten inside curves, by stitching around the opening on this pretty and practical peg bag.

1 Lay the front face downwards and place the hanger centrally across the top, so that the base of the hook lines up with the edge. Draw along the top edge of the hanger, then cut along this line. Fold in half widthways to check the shape is symmetrical and trim as necessary.

2 Following the guideline on the cutting out diagram, draw in a narrow slit with rounded ends, 25cm up from the bottom edge. Work a line of reinforcing machine stitch 3mm outside the line. Using sharp embroidery scissors, cut out the centre to make the opening.

3 Neaten the opening with bias binding, sewn on by hand. So that the binding lies flat at the two ends you will need to pleat the centre and fan out the folded edges into a curve. Stitch the binding to the right side first, then the wrong side.

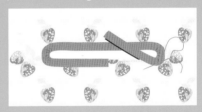

4 Pin the front to the back with wrong sides facing. Trim the top edge of the back so that it is the same shape as the front and tack the two pieces together.

5 Bind the outside edge of the peg bag, as shown on pages 20–21, starting at one side of the top point and remembering to leave a small gap for the hook of the coat hanger. Insert the hanger through the opening and wriggle it about until the hook goes through the gap.

top tip

IF YOU CAN'T FIND A 30CM COAT HANGER, YOU COULD TRY SHORTENING A STANDARD ONE. MEASURE UP AND MARK A CUTTING LINE 15CM FROM THE HOOK ON EACH ARM. CUT THE ENDS OFF CAREFULLY WITH A SMALL HACKSAW AND SMOOTH OFF ANY ROUGH EDGES WITH SANDPAPER.

Lavender
Bags

what you will need...

per bag • 2 x 20cm squares of floral print cotton • 35g dried lavender • 1 small button • 15cm narrow cotton tape • tracing paper • fading pen • matching sewing thread • sewing kit • sewing machine

templates
Large heart and Large bird

Lavender has long been valued both for its fragrance and as a deterrent to moths. These hanging hearts and birds are filled with the dried buds, and will bring their gentle perfume to your wardrobe and linen cupboard. Sew them by hand or machine, for yourself or as presents for friends or family.

1 For the bird bag, trace off the body and wing outlines and cut them out. Pin the body template to the wrong side of the main fabric and draw around the edge. Cut out roughly, leaving about 1cm all round.

2 Cover the wing with the other fabric, following the turned edge appliqué method on page 29. Pin the wing to the right side of the bird making sure it lies in the correct position by holding the fabric up to the light. Slip stitch down.

3 With right sides facing, pin the front to the other fabric and machine stitch around the outline. Leave a 4cm gap along the straight edge at the back.

4 Trim the seam allowance back to 5mm all round. Clip and notch the curves as necessary (see page 23). Press back the allowance on either side of the opening. Turn right side out, ease out the seams and press lightly.

5 Using a teaspoon, fill the bird with lavender, then slip stitch the opening.

6 Fold the tape in half to make a hanging loop and sew the ends to the bird's back, close to the top of the wing. Stitch on the button to make the eye.

7 The heart is made in the same way, with the opening along one straight edge, just above the point. Sew the hanging loop to the centre top.

top tip

SEWING CURVES ON A SMALL SCALE CAN BE FIDDLY, SO I CHEATED! INSTEAD OF CUTTING OUT THE FRONT AND BACK, THEN JOINING THE EDGES, SIMPLY DRAW THE MOTIF ONTO A PIECE OF FABRIC, TACK ANOTHER PIECE TO THE BACK, SEW TOGETHER AROUND THE OUTLINE AND TRIM THE SEAM.

Coat
Hangers

what you will need...

per hanger • 20 x 65cm floral print cotton • wooden coat hanger
• padding: old pairs of tights or jersey top cut into 10cm strips
• 60cm bias binding • matching sewing thread • sewing kit

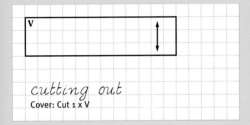

cutting out
Cover: Cut 1 x V

Give your best frocks the special treatment they deserve, and prevent the shoulders from creasing, with these quick-to-make hangers. They have been padded in thrifty style by binding the wooden arms with old pairs of tights: you could also use strips cut from an old t-shirt or jumper.

1 Wrap the padding around the coat hanger. Starting at one end, wind it tightly towards, and then past, the hook. Sew on new lengths when needed and secure the ends with a few stitches.

2 Cut a length of bias binding 2cm longer than the hook. Press under a 5mm turning at one end. Fold in half lengthways and slip stitch the folded end and the long edges together to form a tube. Slide the open end of the tube over the hook and sew the raw ends to the padding.

3 Press a 1cm turning at the short edges and a 2cm turning along the long edges of the cover. Fold in half widthways and mark the centre point.

4 Slip stitch the folds at each short edge. Sew the top edges on the left side together, from the corner to the centre point. Use 5mm running stitches, worked 5mm down from the folds.

5 Slide the coat hanger into the cover. Pull up the thread so that the fabric gathers over the padding. Even out the folds and fasten off the thread. Gather the other side in the same way.

6 Make a bow from the remaining bias binding, trim the ends and stitch to the cover at the base of the hook.

top
tip

A LENGTH OF DOUBLE-SIDED TAPE FIXED ALL THE WAY ACROSS THE ARMS OF THE HANGER WILL STOP THE PADDING FROM SLIPPING ABOUT AS YOU WIND IT IN PLACE.

Lavender
Pillow

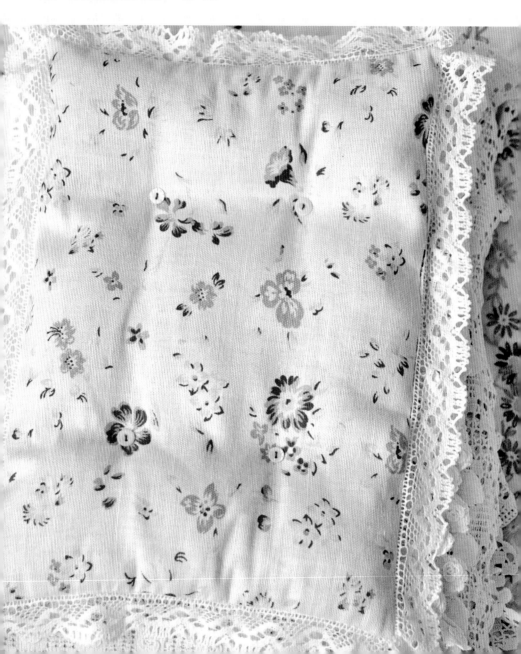

what you will need...

- 35 x 85cm floral print cotton • 300g dried lavender • 1.8m 5cm-wide lace
- 8 x 1cm buttons • matching sewing thread • sewing kit • sewing machine

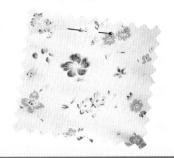

N		N	
x	x	x	x
x	x	x	x

cutting out
Front and Back: Cut 2 x N

Keep this scented pillow on your bed and the soothing qualities of lavender will always bring you the sweetest dreams. To keep the contents evenly distributed and to give it an upholstered look, the front and back have been stitched together at four central points and trimmed with mother of pearl buttons.

1 Mark the four button positions on both front and back pieces, as shown on the diagram above. With right sides facing, pin the two pieces together. Machine stitch, with a 1cm seam allowance. Leave a 10cm gap in the centre of one edge.

2 Press the seam allowance back on either side of the gap. Clip the corners and turn right side out. Ease the corners into shape and press the seams.

3 Fill the bag with lavender by pouring it through a funnel made from a rolled-up sheet of paper. Slip stitch the gap to close.

4 Sew a button onto a marked point at the front, then pass the needle right through to the back, so that it comes out at the corresponding mark. Add another button at the back and stitch the two together through the pillow several times. Do the same at the other three marked points.

5 Pin the lace along one side edge of the pillow. Measure and mark off the next 10cm of lace, then continue pining along the top edge so that the spare lace forms a loop at the corner. Pin the lace to the other two edges, creating a loop at each corner, and then join the ends.

6 Slip stitch the lace in place to each of the seams. Sew a line of running stitches along the straight edge of each loop as you reach it and pull up the thread to gather the lace. Slip stitch the gathers securely to the corners.

top tip YOU CAN INTERPRET THIS PROJECT IN SEVERAL WAYS, BY VARYING THE SIZE AND SHAPE (A SQUARE OR LARGE HEART PERHAPS) OR BY CUTTING THE FRONT AND BACK FROM DIFFERENT FABRICS AND USING VARIOUS TYPES OF BUTTONS ON EACH SIDE TO MAKE THE PILLOW REVERSIBLE.

Quilted
Hottie

what you will need...

- 50 x 60cm paisley or floral print cotton • 50 x 60cm polyester or cotton batting • 50 x 60cm plain cotton for backing • 15 x 40cm contrast floral print cotton for binding • matching sewing thread • 50cm narrow velvet ribbon • 1 x 12mm button • sharp pencil • ruler • sewing kit • sewing machine

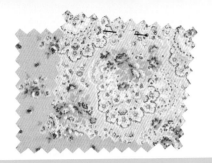

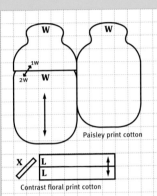

Paisley print cotton

Contrast floral print cotton

drawing up the pattern

Top Front: Use piece W, with line 1w as the bottom edge
Main Front: Use piece W, with line 2w as the top edge
Back: Use piece W, tracing around the entire outline

cutting out

Top Front: Cut 1 from paisley print cotton
Main Front: Cut 1 from paisley print cotton
Back: Cut 1 from paisley print cotton
Binding: Cut 2 x L from contrast floral print cotton
Button Loop: Cut 1 x X from contrast floral print cotton, on the bias
Padding and Backing: Cut 3 x W from cotton batting and backing fabric as given for Top Front, Main Front and Back but adding approximately 3cm all round

This hand-quilted hot water bottle cover, made from pink paisley fabric, was inspired by traditional feather eiderdowns. It is trimmed with a pale turquoise print and fastens with a rouleau loop and a mother of pearl button. Snuggle up close and your hottie will keep you warm and snug on the coldest winter night.

1 You will find all you need to know about hand quilting in the techniques section, so refer back to page 29 for the next two steps. Start by marking a 3cm diamond shaped grid on the right side of each of the three main cover pieces using a ruler and a sharp pencil.

2 Cut out a piece of batting and a piece of backing fabric, each of which is slightly larger all round than the main front panel. Tack the three layers together, quilt along the marked lines and around the outside edges, then trim. Make up the top front and back in the same way.

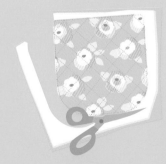

top tip

THE PATTERN DIAGRAM IS FOR A STANDARD SHAPE, BUT CHECK THAT YOUR OWN HOTTIE LIES COMFORTABLY WITHIN THE MARKED SEAM LINE, WITH AT LEAST 2CM EXTRA ALL ROUND. INCREASE THE LENGTH OR WIDTH IF NECESSARY FOR A PERFECT FIT.

Quilted Hottie

3 Using the two longer contrast floral print bias strips, bind the straight edges of the two front panels, as shown on page 20.

4 Make a rouleau loop from the remaining contrast floral print bias strip, following the instructions given on page 25. Trim it down to 6cm in length and fold it in half to form the loop. Sew the ends securely to the wrong side of the top front panel, in the centre of the straight edge.

5 Place the back panel, right side up, on your work surface. Lay the top front panel, face down, across the top so the curved edges line up exactly. Position the main front panel over them both so that the bottom and side edges also match.

6 Pin the three pieces together all round the outside edge.

7 Tack and machine stitch, leaving a 1cm seam allowance. Clip and notch the curves as necessary (see page 23), then turn right side out. Ease the curves into shape.

8 Cut the ribbon in half and tie each piece into a little bow. Cut off the ends diagonally at a sharp angle and sew one bow to each side of the neck of the cover. Sew the button to the centre of the main front panel, just below the buttonhole loop.

top tip → THIS PROJECT IS AN EXCELLENT WAY TO LEARN HOW TO HAND QUILT, BUT IF YOU DON'T FANCY ALL THAT EXTRA STITCHING YOU COULD SIMPLY CUT THE BATTING AND BACKING TO THE SAME SIZE AS THE THREE COVER PIECES AND MAKE A PLAIN BUT PADDED COVER!

Bath
Hat

what you will need...

- 60cm square floral print cotton duck • 60cm square waterproof fabric
- 2m bias binding • 2m narrow lace • 1m hat elastic • 2 small safety pins
- matching sewing thread • sewing kit • sewing machine

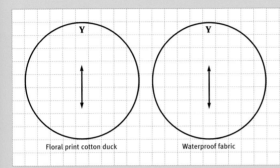

Floral print cotton duck   Waterproof fabric

cutting out

Hat: Cut 1 x Y from floral print cotton duck
Lining: Cut 1 x Y from waterproof fabric

This flowery bath hat is so pretty that you won't ever want to put it away in your bathroom cupboard. It is very easy to make, from a surprisingly large gathered circle of cotton duck or lighter weight cotton, which is lined with waterproof fabric and trimmed with a frill of broderie anglaise.

1 Pin the lining, with wrong sides facing, to the hat and tack them both together all the way round the circumference.

2 Open out one fold of the bias binding and turn under 1cm at the end. With right sides together, tack the binding all the way round the circumference so the unfolded raw edge lies along the outside edge of the hat. You'll find details of how to do this on page 21.

3 When you've got all the way round the hat, trim the other end of the bias binding to 1cm and turn it under so that the two ends butt closely together. Trim the seam allowance back to 3mm.

top tip

I USED A WOVEN SHOWER CURTAIN MATERIAL TO MAKE THE WATERPROOF (BUT NOT WATER-TIGHT!) LINING FOR THE HAT. THIS IS SOFTER AND MORE COMFORTABLE TO WEAR THAN OTHER FABRICS WITH A PLASTICISED FINISH.

Bath
Hat

4 Turn the folded edge of the binding to the wrong side and slip stitch the fold along the curved seam line.

5 Sew the straight edge of the broderie anglaise or lace to the right side of the hat along the bottom edge of the binding, with the scalloped edge facing outwards. Trim and seam the two ends.

6 Tie the elastic securely to a safety pin. Use another pin to fasten the loose end of the elastic close to the gap in the binding, so that it won't disappear as you gather up the hat.

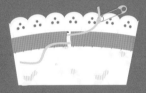

7 Thread the elastic through the gap and around the binding, pulling it up as you go. Check that you have a comfortable fit, then knot and stitch the ends together. Trim the elastic to 2cm and slide the knot so that it is hidden within the binding.

top tip

THE MORE MINIMALIST AMONGST YOU MAY WANT TO OMIT
THE LACE TRIMMING AND OPT FOR A PLAINER LOOK.

what you will need...

for the Pincushion • 24 x 13cm floral print cotton duck • 25cm narrow ribbon
• polyester toy filling • matching sewing thread • sewing kit • sewing machine
for the Needlecase • 40 x 35cm floral print cotton duck • 30cm square felt
• bondaweb • thin card • pinking shears • press stud • matching sewing thread
• sewing kit • sewing machine

cutting out

Needlecase Cover: Cut 1 x Z from card and 1 x Z from
   cotton duck, adding approximately 1cm all round
Needlecase Pages: Cut 1 x 1Z, 1 x 2Z and 1 x 3Z
   from felt, using pinking shears
Tab: Cut 2 x 4Z from cotton duck

template

Small heart

If you've got the sewing bug, you'll need plenty of different needles for plain stitching, embroidery and quilting. Store them safely in the felt pages of this handy needlcase, then make the adorable heart-shaped pincushion to match. However, don't put your needles in the pincushion – they may disappear into the filling!

1 To make the pincushion, trace round the small heart template onto the wrong side of the floral print cotton duck. Cut out roughly, 1cm from the drawn line. Cut another piece of fabric the same size and tack the two together with right sides facing.

2 Machine stitch around the outline, leaving a 4cm gap in one straight side. Trim the seam allowance back to 6mm. Clip and notch the curves as necessary (see page 23). Press the seam allowance back on both sides of the gap and turn right side out. Ease the curves into shape.

3 Stuff the pincushion with your chosen filling, packing it down firmly through the gap. Close the gap with slip stitch.

4 Tie the velvet ribbon into a small bow and trim the ends into fishtails. Sew the ribbon bow in place on the centre top of the finished heart pincushion.

top tip

ALTERNATIVE PINCUSHION FILLINGS OVER THE YEARS HAVE INCLUDED SAWDUST; CLEAN SHEEP'S FLEECE WHICH CONTAINS NATURAL LANOLIN; COFFEE GROUNDS TO PREVENT RUST, AND SAND OR EMERY POWDER WHICH GIVE YOU A HEAVIER CUSHION AND KEEP THE POINTS SHARP.

Pincushion & Needlecase

1 To make the needlecase, cut a rectangle of Bondaweb 1cm larger on each side than the thin card cover. Iron this to the floral print fabric and cut out around the edge. Peel off the backing paper.

2 Place the needlecase cover on your ironing board with the Bondaweb facing upwards, then position the card centrally on top.

3 Fold the corners of the fabric cover over the card, gently pressing them down in turn with the tip of your iron. Now fold the sides over and iron each one so that the corners are neatly mitred.

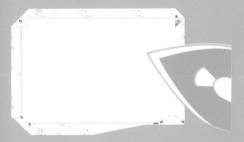

4 Turn the needlecase cover the other way up and, protecting the surface with a piece of spare fabric, iron it gently so the fabric fuses onto the card.

5 Stitch the recessed half of the press stud halfway down the right side, 2cm in from the edge.

6 Stitch the other half of the press stud to the round end of one tab, on the right side. Tack and machine the two tabs together around the long and curved edges, leaving a 5mm seam allowance. Notch the allowance around the curve and turn right side out.

7 Glue the sewn tab half way down the right edge of the needlecase, with the press stud facing upwards.

8 Trace the cover lining (1Z) onto the paper side of the Bondaweb. Cut out roughly, then iron it onto the felt. Cut along the pencil line using pinking shears.

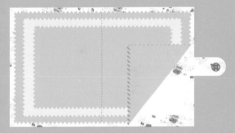

9 Pin the other two pages centrally on top and machine stitch together down the centre. Peel off the backing paper from the first page, then press it onto the cover.

top tip BUY SEVERAL PACKETS OF NEEDLES IN VARIOUS SHAPES AND SIZES AND TRANSFER THEM TO YOUR COMPLETED NEEDLECASE, KEEPING ONE TYPE ON EACH FELT PAGE. YOU'LL ALSO FIND IT USEFUL TO ADD A FEW ASSORTED SAFETY PINS AND PERHAPS A NEEDLE THREADER.

Knitting
Bag

what you will need...

- selection of dress weight cotton • old envelopes and recycled paper • 55 x 125cm floral print cotton for lining
- 2 round bag handles • matching sewing thread • sewing kit
- sewing machine

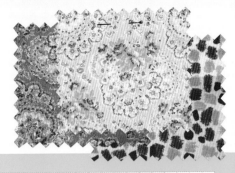

template
Hexagon

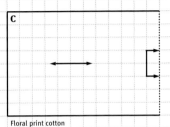

Floral print cotton

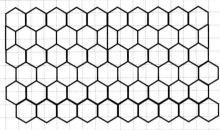

Layout for Hexagons and Half hexagons

cutting out

Lining: Cut 1 x C from floral print cotton, on the fold

Hexagon patchwork, with its characteristic honeycomb pattern, was hugely popular in Victorian times and once again in the Seventies, when it was used to create countless bedcovers and cushions. It's high time for another revival of this absorbing hand technique: start off with this useful knitting bag.

1 Make 60 paper hexagons using the template as a guide, and cut two of them in half, from point to point.

2 Cut out a piece of fabric 1cm larger all round than the hexagon. Don't worry about being too accurate – just make sure it is big enough to cover the template comfortably.

3 Pin a paper hexagon centrally to the wrong side of the cut fabric. Turning down one edge at a time and making a neat fold at each angle, tack the surplus fabric to the paper template.

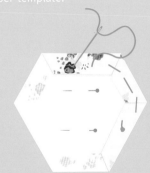

top tip

IF YOU WANT YOUR DESIGN TO HAVE AN OVERALL THEME, KEEP TO A LIMITED COLOUR PALETTE, AS I DID. FOR A MORE RANDOM, HAPHAZARD LOOK, JUST GO FOR ALL THE FABRICS YOU CAN FIND. TAKE A LOOK AT THE FABULOUS VINTAGE BEDSPREAD ON PAGES 90–91 TO SEE WHAT I MEAN!

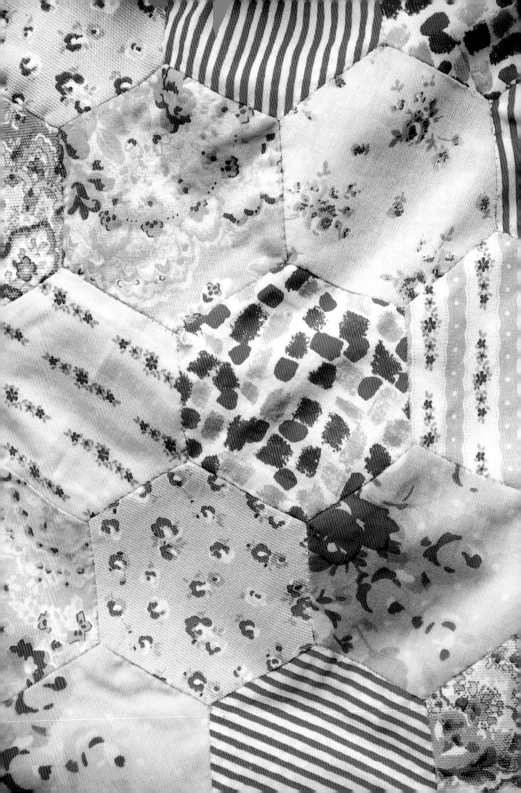

Knitting Bag

4 Join the first two patches by lining them up with right sides facing, and slip stitching through two adjacent edges. Make small, closely spaced stitches and pass the needle through the fabric only, not the paper templates. Sew two sides of a third hexagon into the angle between the first two.

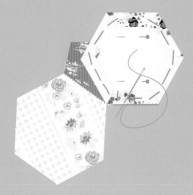

5 Continue building up all of the patches into a mosaic, following the layout diagram. Stitch the first 40 together in four staggered rows of ten.

6 Sew a half-hexagon at each end of the fifth row and, working inwards, add four more hexagons to each side and two more half-hexagons in the centre, but don't join these two patches together.

7 For the sixth row, sew five hexagons at each end without joining the middle two in the centre.

8 Press the finished patchwork and fold it in half with right sides facing. Join the edges of the hexagons at the ends of the bottom three rows, to make the bag.

9 Unpick all the papers (you can reuse these for another project). Trim a shallow triangle from the edge of each hexagon on the top and bottom rows to make straight edges, taking care not to cut into the seams.

10 Fold the bag, wrong side out, so that the openings lie at the side edges. Pin the front and back together along the bottom edge and machine stitch, leaving a 1cm seam allowance. Turn right side out.

top tip → PATCHWORK ORIGINATED AT A TIME WHEN NEW MATERIALS WERE EXPENSIVE AND OFTEN HARD TO COME BY. MAINTAIN THE TRADITION – AND YOUR GREEN CREDENTIALS – BY SAVING ALL YOUR OFFCUTS, ALONG WITH YOUR FAMILY'S OLD GARMENTS, TO MAKE YOUR HEXAGONS.

Knitting Bag

11 Fold the lining in half lengthways, with right sides facing, and pin the side edges together. Make a 25cm seam, from the corner upwards on each side, 5cm from the edge. Trim 10cm from the top edge. Press down the remaining seam allowances at the sides, then press under 1cm along the top edges.

12 Slip the lining inside the bag. Pin and slip stitch the folded side edges to the patchwork. Machine stitch the top edge of the patchwork to the lining at the front and back, where they meet.

13 Fold the top edge of the front lining over to the bag, passing it through the first handle. Pin the folded edge to the patchwork as you go, just below the line of machine stitching. Slip stitch in place, then repeat at the back.

top tip

KNITTING BAG HANDLES COME IN VARIOUS SHAPES AND SIZES. I LIKED THESE BOUND RED RINGS, BUT LOOK OUT AT YOUR LOCAL HABERDASHERS OR SEARCH ONLINE FOR WOODEN, BAMBOO OR BRIGHT PLASTIC VERSIONS.

Knitting
Needle Case

what you will need...

- 45 x 50cm floral print cotton • 45 x 55cm spotted cotton for lining
- 45cm nylon zip • 75cm bias binding • matching sewing thread
- sewing kit • sewing machine

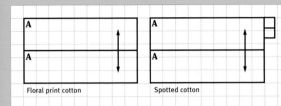

Floral print cotton   Spotted cotton

cutting out

Bag: Cut 2 x A from floral print cotton
Lining: Cut 2 x A from spotted cotton
Zip cover: Cut 2 x 4cm squares from
    spotted cotton

Don't be put off by the idea of sewing in a zip – it's not nearly as complicated as you might think! I chose a bright red one for this long thin knitting needle case, which echoes the colour of the roses in the main floral print and stands out well against the spotty lining.

1 With right sides facing, pin and machine stitch one long edge of a lining piece to a bag piece, with a 5mm allowance. Press the seam away from the lining.

2 Fold along the seam line with wrong sides together, and press so that 5mm of the lining is visible above the top edge of the bag. Trim the bottom edge of the front so that it is the same depth as the lining. Join the other two pieces in the same way.

3 Fold the two small squares in half. Tack one across each end of the closed zip, with the folds facing inwards. Double check the length against the bag and adjust if necessary.

4 Open the zip. Tack one side of the bag to one side of the zip so that the teeth lie just below the top edge. Do the same on the other side and close the zip.

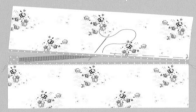

5 Fit a zip foot to your sewing machine and, from the right side, machine stitch the zip to the bag, 3mm below the seam line. Sew across the zip at each end, 1cm from the edge.

6 Fold the bag with right sides facing, so that the zip lies in the middle. Tack the side and bottom edges together, then machine stitch leaving a 1cm seam. Trim the allowance to 4mm and bind to neaten (see page 20). Turn case right side out.

top tip

THE FINISHED SIZE OF 43CM MEANS THAT THIS BAG IS LONG ENOUGH FOR MOST STANDARD KNITTING NEEDLES, BUT IF YOU HAVE GOT SOME EXTRA BIG PAIRS AMONGST YOUR COLLECTION, INCREASE THE LENGTH ACCORDINGLY SO THAT THEY WILL FIT IN.

Girl's Apron

what you will need...

• 50cm square strawberry print cotton duck • 40 x 85cm spotted cotton duck • matching sewing thread • sewing kit • sewing machine

template
Large heart

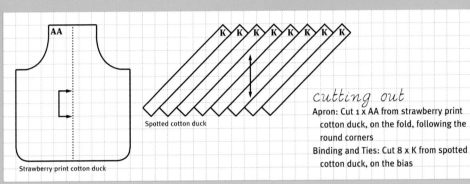

AA

Strawberry print cotton duck

Spotted cotton duck

K K K K K K K K

cutting out

Apron: Cut 1 x AA from strawberry print cotton duck, on the fold, following the round corners

Binding and Ties: Cut 8 x K from spotted cotton duck, on the bias

It's not always easy to keep children clean when they're in the kitchen, but here are two aprons that may help! The girl's version has contrasting bound edges whilst the boy's one overleaf is quicker to make and a perfect beginner's project. Swap the fabrics as you wish, to suit your sewing skills and your child.

1 You'll find all you need to know about bias binding on pages 20-21. Following the steps, join the spotted strips, then use them to bind around the neck and the lower half of the apron. Top stitch 3mm from the edge.

2 Mark a point 25cm away from the centre of the remaining binding. This gives you the size of the neck loop, which you can adjust as necessary.

3 Open out one fold of the binding and pin the first mark to the left edge of the neck, with raw edges together. Pin and sew the binding to the apron, following the instructions for inside curves. Do the same at the other side.

4 Tack the two folded edges of the binding together around the neck loop.

5 Trim the ties to the same length, and press under 1cm at each end. Tack the folded edges together. Starting at the end of one tie, and finishing at the other, top stitch all the way along the binding, 3mm from the edge.

6 Make the pocket from the remaining spotted fabric, as for steps 1 and 2 of the pincushion on page 79. Slip stitch the gap and press. Pin the pocket to the apron and sew down along the straight edges with neat top stitches.

top tip → GIVE YOUR APRON A CO-ORDINATED LOOK BY PICKING OUT A COLOUR FROM THE MAIN FABRIC TO USE FOR THE POCKET AND BINDING. I MATCHED THE BLUE SPOT FABRIC TO THE STRAWBERRY FLOWERS, AND AS A BONUS, THE SPOTS ECHO THE SEED PATTERN ON THE RED FRUIT.

Boy's
Apron

what you will need...

- 60 x 50cm cowboy print dress weight cotton • 60 x 50cm white cotton
- 45 x 50cm red cotton • bondaweb • stranded cotton embroidery thread
in matching colours • 2 D-rings • matching sewing thread • sewing kit
- sewing machine

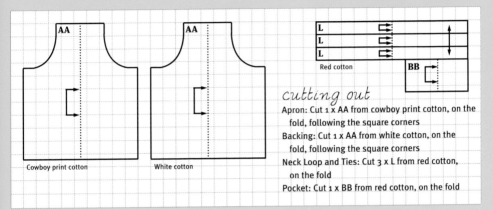

Cowboy print cotton

White cotton

Red cotton

cutting out

Apron: Cut 1 x AA from cowboy print cotton, on the
fold, following the square corners

Backing: Cut 1 x AA from white cotton, on the
fold, following the square corners

Neck Loop and Ties: Cut 3 x L from red cotton,
on the fold

Pocket: Cut 1 x BB from red cotton, on the fold

Curved seams, like those on either side of
the bib, can be tricky if you have to hem or
bind them, but this apron uses a cheat's
way to avoid complicated techniques.

1 Pin the front to the lining around the side
and bottom edges, with right sides facing.
Seam together, 1cm from the edge, leaving
the neck open. Clip and notch the curves as
necessary (see page 23). Turn right side out.
Press under the seam allowance at the neck
and slip stitch the edges together.

2 Make a 1cm double seam along the top of
the pocket and top stitch both edges. Press
under a 1cm seam at the other sides, so
that the fabric is turned to the back.

3 Press the pocket in half lengthways to
mark the centre. Cut a few motifs from the

offcuts and appliqué them with Bondaweb
(see page 28). Edge each shape with straight
stitches. Embroider the lassoes in chain
stitch and the grass with straight stitches.

4 Sew the pocket in place and add a line
of stitching down the centre.

5 Make two red strips into ties, as on page
27, neatening both ends. Sew one to each
side of the waist with reinforcing stitching.

6 Cut 10cm from the third strip, Make a tie
from each piece. Slip the short tie through
the D-rings. Fold in half and stitch the ends
to the left corner of
neck edge as before.
Sew the other tie to
the right corner. Loop
end through the rings.

THE COMIC STRIP COWBOYS ARE GREAT FUN TO DO AND TO WEAR. IF YOU ARE MAKING A
MORE GIRLY APRON YOU COULD MAKE A SIMILAR POCKET WITH LEAVES AND BLOOMS
CUT FROM FLOWERED FABRIC, OR USE ONE OF THE MOTIFS AT THE BACK OF THE BOOK
FOR A SIMPLER DESIGN.

what you will need...

• bondaweb • 35 x 45cm red star print cotton duck • 20 x 80cm blue spotted cotton duck • scraps of floral print and green cotton • small button • matching sewing thread • 1m piping cord • 18 x 26cm block of wood, padded with wadding on one side • hammer and tacks or staplegun • sewing kit

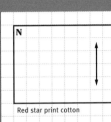

N

Red star print cotton

H

Blue spotted cotton

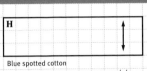

template
Stanley

cutting out
Background: Cut 1 x N from star print cotton
Piping: Cut 1 x H from blue spotted cotton

Stanley, my Lakeland Terrier, has become something of a design icon in his own right. He even has a special fabric to himself, called 'Mini Stanley'. This iron-on appliqué picture is based on one of the motifs in that print and shows him proudly sporting his best vintage floral coat and a spotty collar.

1 Using the template, trace the main Stanley outline onto Bondaweb, reversing the image if you wish him to face to the right. Following the steps on page 28, cut him out from the blue spotted fabric, and iron him centrally onto the red star print fabric.

2 Add a matching ear, then make his collar from green spotted fabric and his coat from the floral print. Sew on the button for his eye.

3 Place the finished appliqué face downwards and position the wooden block on top, making sure that it lies centrally over Stanley. Turn back the top edge and tack or staple it onto the wood. Now turn back the opposite edge, stretching it slightly and fix that down too. Secure the side edges in the same way.

4 To make the piping, press the strip of spotted fabric in half lengthways and cut along the fold. Sew the two pieces together and press the seam open, then cover the cord as shown on page 23.

5 Tack the piping around the edge of the fabric-covered block, joining the round. Tack or staple the loose fabric to the back.

top tip

LOOK OUT FOR A CHARACTERFUL OLD CARVED FRAME AS AN ALTERNATIVE WAY TO DISPLAY YOUR PICTURE: IT DOESN'T MATTER IF THE GLASS IS MISSING OR IF THERE ARE A FEW KNOCKS AND CHIPS AS YOU CAN EASILY REVIVE THE WOODWORK WITH A COAT OR TWO OF PAINT.

Bird
Mobile

what you will need...

- 45cm square mini floral print cotton • scraps of other fabrics
- polyester toy filling • black 3mm rocaille beads • strong white
beading thread • two 25cm garden sticks • curtain ring or split ring
- matching sewing thread • sewing kit • sewing machine

template
Small bird

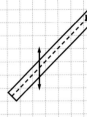

cutting out
Binding: Cut 1 x K from mini floral print cotton,
on the bias. Cut the strip in half lengthways

Mix and match your leftover scraps of fabric to make these little bobbing birds, switching them around on wings and bodies. A jumble of mini prints always works well, so I chose three favourites, featuring roses, buds and stars, then added a paisley and a vintage rose print in the same colour palette.

1 Using the template, trace the bird's body and wing outlines onto paper and cut out. Draw round the body template onto the wrong side of a piece of fabric. Cut out roughly and, with right sides facing, pin to a second piece of the same fabric. Tack close to the outline.

2 Stitch around the outline, leaving a 3cm gap along the back. The lavender bird diagram on page 65 will show you how to do this.

3 Cut out, leaving a 6mm seam allowance. Press back the allowance along the opening, then clip and notch the curves. Turn right side out, stuff gently with toy filling and close the gap with slip stitch. Sew a bead to each side of the head for the eyes.

4 Make two wings in the same way. Turn right side out, press and slip stitch to the finished bird.

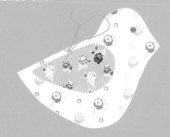

 top tip

GIVE EACH OF YOUR FLOCK ITS OWN INDIVIDUAL CHARACTER
BY VARYING THE POSITION OF THE HANGING THREADS, AND
THE ANGLE AT WHICH YOU SEW THE WINGS.

Bird
Mobile

5 Bind each stick with a bias strip, wrapping it diagonally, and stitching down the ends. Hold them together in a cross, and bind the centre with thread or a very narrow strip of fabric. A few stitches, worked through the bindings, will keep the sticks securely fixed.

6 Stitch a 30cm length of beading thread to the end of each arm of the cross and knot the loose ends together. Tie the ends to the ring and trim.

7 Sew a length of beading thread to the back of each bird. Stitch the loose ends to the centre and tips of the cross. Hang each one of them at a different length, making sure the centre bird has the longest thread.

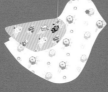

top tip → THE BIRDS ARE GOING TO APPEAL TO EVERYBODY WHO SEES THEM, BUT FOR SAFETY'S SAKE, PLEASE KEEP THE MOBILE WELL OUT OF THE REACH OF THE SMALLEST MEMBERS OF YOUR FAMILY.

Stanley
Toy

what you will need...

- 20cm square 'Stanley' print cotton • 20cm blue spotted cotton
- 1m red ricrac • tiny button • scraps of red and green felt • green
embroidery thread • filling • sewing kit

template
Stanley

Lucky mascot Stanley is one of the smallest projects in the book, but – as you may expect – I have to admit that it is my favourite! He's stitched completely by hand, and can be made in an afternoon. This pet print was just the right fabric to use, but you could vary the look with spots on both sides or a mini floral design.

1 Cut out a paper Stanley template. Pin to the wrong side of the printed fabric so that his nose is pointing left. Trim the seam to 5mm, then notch and clip as shown on page 23. Fold the seam allowance over and tack it to the paper. Press and remove the paper.

2 Make the back in the same way, with Stanley facing to the right. Slip stitch the ricrac around the edge, so that the scallops project beyond the fold.

3 Pin the front to the back, sandwiching the ricrac between the two. Slip stitch together, leaving a gap along Stanley's tummy. Stuff the body with your chosen filling, a spoonful at a time, then close the gap.

4 Cut out the ear template and make two shapes from printed fabric as for the body. Slip stitch them together and sew in place along the top edge only. Add a narrow strip of felt for the collar.

5 To make his nametag, write 'Stan' on the red felt and work tiny back stitches over the letters using the green embroidery thread. Cut out, using a coin to give you a neat circle, and sew the tag to the collar. Finish off with a tiny button for Stanley's eye.

top → BEAN BAGS ARE USUALLY STUFFED WITH LENTILS OR RICE, TO GIVE THEIR
tip CHARACTERISTIC WEIGHT AND TEXTURE. SUCH FILLINGS, HOWEVER, WON'T STAND
UP TO THE DAMP SO YOU COULD USE THE NEWER ALTERNATIVE – SPECIALLY MADE
NYLON BEADS AVAILABLE FROM GOOD CRAFT SUPPLIERS.

Cot
Quilt

what you will need...

• 65 x 140cm floral print cotton duck • 45 x 140cm pink spotted cotton duck • 55 x 140cm blue spotted cotton duck • 80 x 120cm cotton duck • 80 x 120cm backing fabric • sewing kit • sewing machine • twin needle for machine (optional)

templates

Elephant and Small bird

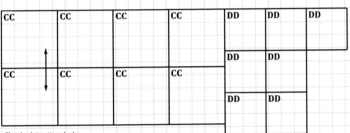

Floral print cotton duck

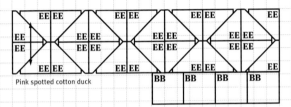

Pink spotted cotton duck

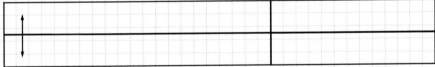

Blue spotted cotton duck

drawing up the pattern

Top and Bottom Borders: Using A as a width guide, cut 2 x 12.5 x 105cm strips
Side Borders: Using A as a width guide, cut 2 x 65cm strips

cutting out

Elephant blocks: Cut 8 x CC from floral print cotton
Bird blocks: Cut 7 x DD from floral print cotton and 28 EE from pink spotted cotton
Corner Squares: Cut 4 x BB from pink spotted cotton
Top and Bottom Borders: Cut 2 from blue spotted cotton
Side Borders: Cut 2 from blue spotted cotton

top
tip

DEPENDING ON YOUR SKILL AND PATIENCE YOU CAN OMIT THE TWIN STITCHING AND CROSS STITCHES, AND INSTEAD HAND QUILT THE ENTIRE SURFACE OF THE PATCHWORK, OUTLINING EACH OF THE BLOCKS, AND IF YOU'VE TIME, THE ELEPHANTS AND THE BIRDS.

Cot Quilt

Here are the birds again, this time sitting alongside their elephant friends on a charming cot quilt. The time and skill involved in stitching patchwork makes it a labour of love, so this makes a wonderful gift for a newborn. The pink and blue colour scheme makes it suitable for a girl or a boy.

The seam allowance throughout is 1cm

1 Referring to page 28, cut out eight Bondaweb elephants from blue spotted fabric, four facing right and four left. Iron them centrally onto the large squares. Add blue tails and pink ears and eyes. Straight stitch around each shape, with matching thread. Embroider the eyes with cross stitches.

2 Fix a blue bird to each small square, three facing right and four facing left. Give each one a pink wing and an embroidered eye. Sew a pink triangle to each side of the square and press the seams inwards.

3 With right sides facing, pin the blocks together in five rows of three: three rows with the elephants on the outside, facing inwards, and two rows with the birds at the outside, also looking inwards. Machine stitch together.

4 Press all the seams towards the elephant blocks, then join the five rows together matching the seams. Fit the twin needle to your machine and work a line of double stitching over each long seam.

5 Sew the side borders to the quilt and press the seams open. Sew the remaining four spotted squares to each end of the top and bottom borders. Press the seams open, then pin and stitch in place, matching the seams at the corner squares.

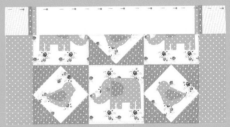

6 Press seams open and machine stitch along the top and bottom edges. Press a 1cm turning along each outside edge.

7 Lay out the quilt with the right side facing downwards. Place the batting centrally across it, with backing fabric on top. Pin the three layers together. Secure the layers with a cross stitch across the corners of each block.

8 Finish off by turning the surplus fabric to the back, folding the corners over neatly. Pin down and slip stitch the fold to the backing.

top tip

ANYTHING THAT COMES INTO CONTACT WITH BABIES AND SMALL CHILDREN WILL UNDOUBTEDLY NEED TO BE LAUNDERED AT REGULAR INTERVALS, SO DON'T FORGET TO WASH AND PRESS YOUR FABRIC BEFORE YOU START TO AVOID ANY SHRINKAGE OR COLOUR RUNS AT A LATER DATE.

Heart
Quilt

what you will need...

• 145 x 140cm white cotton • 65 x 125cm printed cotton for the border
• 75 x 140cm each of three different printed cottons • 150 x 180cm
printed cotton for the backing (join as necessary) • 150 x 180cm
cotton batting • 3m x 44cm-wide bondaweb • quilter's safety pins
(optional) • quilting thread • matching sewing thread • sewing kit
• sewing machine

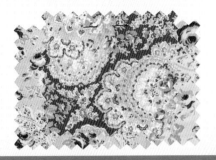

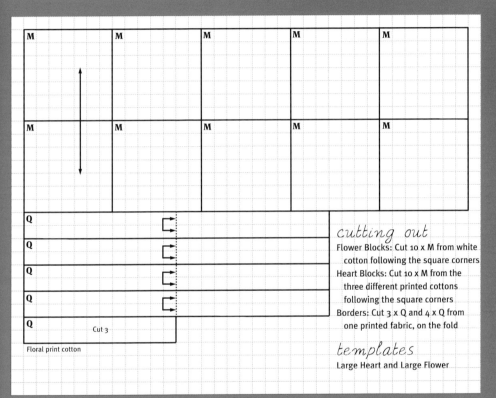

| M | M | M | M | M |
| M | M | M | M | M |

Q ⊏→
Q ⊏→
Q ⊏→
Q ⊏→
Q   Cut 3

Floral print cotton

cutting out

Flower Blocks: Cut 10 x M from white
   cotton following the square corners
Heart Blocks: Cut 10 x M from the
   three different printed cottons
   following the square corners
Borders: Cut 3 x Q and 4 x Q from
   one printed fabric, on the fold

templates

Large Heart and Large Flower

Making an appliqué quilt on the scale of
this stunning hearts and flowers design,
has always been a major undertaking, but
contemporary techniques mean that it will
take much less time than you may expect!
You will find detailed step-by-step
instructions for iron-on appliqué on page 28.

1 To make a flower block, using the Large
Flower template, cut one flower, two leaves
and one stalk, each from a different print.
Iron onto a square of white cotton. Select a
new combination for each of the ten blocks.
Edge the shapes with straight stitch, worked
in matching thread.

top
tip →

THE FINISHED QUILT MEASURES 142 X 175CM – THE PERFECT SIZE TO GO OVER A
STANDARD SINGLE BED. ADD ONE OR MORE ROWS OF SQUARES TO THE SIDE EDGE IF YOU
NEED TO MAKE IT WIDE ENOUGH FOR A QUEEN, DOUBLE OR A EVEN KING-SIZED BED.

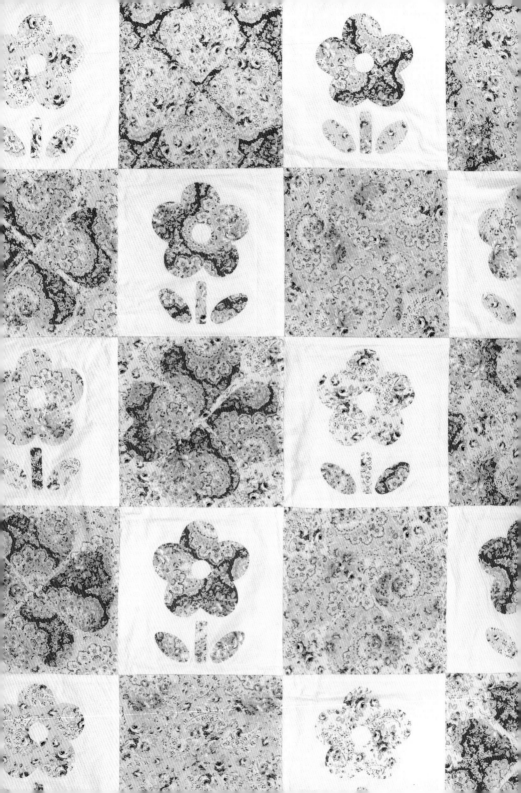

Heart Quilt

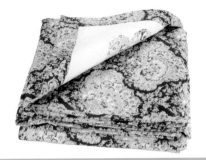

2 Appliqué four matching hearts to each of the print squares, positioning them centrally, with points facing inwards. Mix and match the prints so all ten blocks look different.

3 Alternating hearts and flowers, arrange the completed blocks in five rows of four, in a chequerboard pattern.

4 Join the horizontal rows, leaving a 1cm seam allowance. Press all the seams open. Pin the top two rows together, matching the seams exactly, then stitch 1cm from the edge. Press seams open. Join the other three rows in the same way.

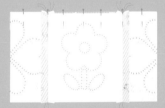

5 Spread out the backing, face downwards. Lay the wadding on top, then place the quilt top centrally over the two. Starting from the centre, pin or tack all three layers together. Firstly work out towards the four corners, then to the midpoint of each side.

6 Work a line of tacking along the centre of each row of blocks, so you end up with a grid across the surface, with a cross joining the corners. Sew or pin all round the outside edge.

7 Using quilting thread and a short needle, stitch along each seam line: quilters call this 'stitching in the ditch'. If sewing by machine use a 'walking foot' to prevent puckering. Trim backing and batting to 5cm all round.

8 Leaving a 1cm allowance, join all the border strips and press the seams open. Cut two 170cm lengths and press under a 1cm turning along one long edge of each.

9 With right sides facing and raw edges together, stitch to side edges of patchwork, leaving 2cm overlapping the border at each end. Press outwards. Add two 145cm top and bottom borders in the same way.

10 Pin the overlapping border to the back of the quilt and slip stitch in place along the folded edges.

top tip

I CHOSE ALL THREE DIFFERENT VERSIONS OF MY VINTAGE-INSPIRED 'ROSE PAISLEY' PRINT TO MAKE THIS QUILT. THIS UNEXPECTED COMBINATION GIVES A UNIQUE AND SUBTLE APPEARANCE TO THE HEART BLOCKS, WHERE THE COLOURS BLEND HARMONIOUSLY.

Aeroplane
Blanket

what you will need...

• 160cm square fleece fabric • 2 skeins of red tapestry yarn • large crewel
needle • 15 x 20cm each red, green, blue and yellow felt • bondaweb
• matching sewing thread • sewing kit

template
Aeroplane

Working with felt appeals to children and
adults alike because it is so quick and
easy to use. It comes in bright primary
colours and has the advantage of not
fraying, even when cut into intricate shapes.
This cosy blanket is a great project to make
together, as a way to learn about appliqué
and stitching.

1 Turn up and tack down a 1cm double hem
all round the outside edge of the fleece.

2 Using a large crewel needle threaded with
tapestry yarn, work a round of blanket stitch
to keep the hem in place.

3 Following the steps for iron-on appliqué
on page 28, trace off the various parts of
the aeroplanes onto Bondaweb, reversing
one of the motis. You can follow the colours
I used or make up your own variation.

4 Lightly iron down the bodies of the
aircraft first, using a pressing cloth to
protect the surface of the felt and fleece.
Add the windows, wings and tails.

5 Finish off by stitching around each
individual shape with small straight stitches
in thread to match each of the different
colours of felt.

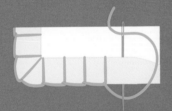

top
tip

I APPLIQUED THIS TRIO OF JET LINERS ONTO A BACKGROUND OF SOFT FLEECE,
BUT THEY WOULD ALSO CHEER UP AN OLD WOOLLEN BLANKET OR PLAIN
BEDCOVER. IF YOU HAVE AN AVIATION ENTHUSIAST IN THE FAMILY, YOU COULD
ADD A WHOLE FLEET TO A SET OF MATCHING CUSHIONS.

Beanie
Cushion

what you will need...

• 1m x 130cm calico • 7 litres of polystyrene beads • 1m x 130cm printed cotton • 30cm zip • 15 x 25cm spotted cotton • matching sewing thread • sewing kit • sewing machine

drawing up the pattern

Reinforcement: Use piece GG, with line 1gg as one short edge

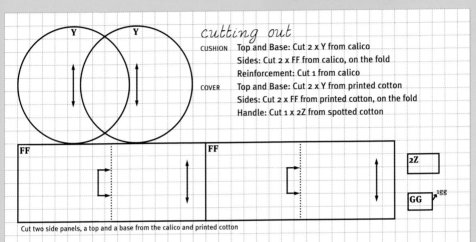

cutting out

CUSHION	Top and Base: Cut 2 x Y from calico
	Sides: Cut 2 x FF from calico, on the fold
	Reinforcement: Cut 1 from calico
COVER	Top and Base: Cut 2 x Y from printed cotton
	Sides: Cut 2 x FF from printed cotton, on the fold
	Handle: Cut 1 x 2Z from spotted cotton

Cut two side panels, a top and a base from the calico and printed cotton

Squashy bean bags are fun to have in bedrooms or playrooms. This one has a toddler-sized handle, so its young owner can drag it from place to place, then nestle down. The cover is bound to get grubby, so I inserted a zip for easy removal.

The seam allowance throughout is 2cm

1 Join the short edges of the calico sides, leaving a 20cm gap in one seam. Press the seams open and press back the unstitched allowance. Add the top and base, as shown on page 23. Turn right side out, fill with beads and join the gap.

2 Make up the handle as on page 27, then join the ends and press the seam open. Pin

to the centre of the cover top, on the right side. Pin the reinforcement to the wrong side, directly behind the handle. Machine stitch the handle in place.

3 Press under 3cm along one left and one right edge of the side panels. Sew the zip between these edges (see page 25) and slip stitch the folds together for 2.5cm at each end.

4 Open the zip and add top and base as before. Turn right sides out and press lightly. Insert the cushion and do up the zip.

top tip

GETTING THE FILLED CUSHION INSIDE THE COVER MAY PROVE TO BE A BIT OF A STRUGGLE, BUT I PROMISE YOU THAT IT WILL GO IN EVENTUALLY! EASE THE BEADS THROUGH THE OPEN ZIP AND MAKE SURE THAT THE CUSHION IS THE RIGHT WAY UP.

Duffel
Bag

what you will need...

- 50 x 110cm print cotton duck • 30cm square striped cotton duck
- 20cm square red felt • scraps of green and blue felt • bondaweb
- 1m thick cotton cord • matching sewing thread • sewing kit
- sewing machine

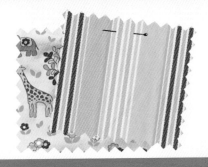

template
Elephant

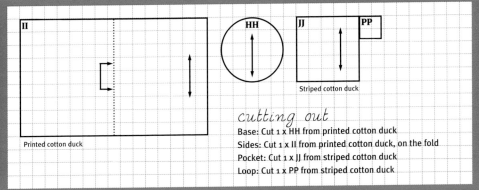

Printed cotton duck

Striped cotton duck

cutting out

Base: Cut 1 x HH from printed cotton duck
Sides: Cut 1 x II from printed cotton duck, on the fold
Pocket: Cut 1 x JJ from striped cotton duck
Loop: Cut 1 x PP from striped cotton duck

Whether it's sports kit, swimming towels, school books or holiday clothes, busy families always seem to have endless amounts of 'stuff' to move around from place to place. Make everybody's life a little easier with this roomy drawstring duffel, which should appeal to even the coolest kids!

The seam allowance throughout is 1.5cm

1 As shown on page 28, appliqué the felt motif to the pocket and edge the main pieces with satin stitch. I added a green blanket to the basic design, to match those on the 'Circus Elephant' fabric.

2 Sew a 1cm double hem at the top of the pocket, then press under a 1cm turning along the other three edges.

3 Zigzag the sides of the side panel. Sew the completed pocket to the centre, 10cm up from the bottom edge. Reinforce the seams at the top corners with extra stitches.

4 Mark a point 10cm down from the top corner on each side edge. Press a 1cm then a 5cm turning along the top edge. Unfold the second turning and with right sides facing, pin the side edges together from the marked points to the bottom corner. Machine stitch this part of the seam, reinforcing both ends, and press open.

top tip IF YOU WOULD LIKE TO MAKE A SMALLER VERSION OF THIS BAG, FOR A YOUNGER CHILD PERHAPS, YOU COULD EASILY ADAPT THE BOLSTER CUSHION PATTERN. SHORTEN THE WIDTH OF THE RECTANGLE TO THE HEIGHT REQUIRED, REMEMBERING TO INCLUDE AN EXTRA 6CM FOR THE CASING.

Duffel Bag

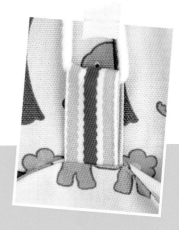

5 Refold the second turning and pin it to the top edge of the bag to make the drawstring casing. Machine stitch close to the fold.

6 Fold the loop fabric in half, then press the side edges to the centre crease and top stitch. Fold in half lengthways and stitch both ends to the bottom of the seam, on the right side.

7 Clip the circular base and sides, following the instructions on page 23 and pin together with right sides facing.

8 Seam with two rounds of machine stitch. Trim the allowance back to about 8mm and zigzag to neaten. Turn the bag right side out.

9 Fasten one end of the cord to a safety pin and thread it through the drawstring casing. Take the pin through the loop, then stitch the ends of the cord securely together.

top tip → I DECORATED THE POCKET WITH A BRIGHTLY COLOURED ELEPHANT, TO GO WITH THE FABRIC I CHOSE FOR THE BAGS. IF YOU ARE GOING TO USE A DIFFERENT PRINT YOU COULD SELECT EITHER THE FLOWER, BIRD OR AEROPLANE MOTIFS AS AN ALTERNATIVE.

Shoulder
Bag

what you will need...

- 60 x 70cm floral print cotton duck • matching sewing thread • three 2cm buttons
- matching stranded embroidery thread • sewing kit • sewing machine

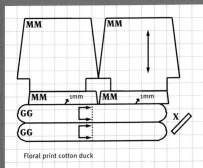

Floral print cotton duck

drawing up the pattern

Facing: Use piece MM, with line 1mm as the bottom edge

cutting out

Front and Back: Cut 2 x MM
Facing: Cut 2
Strap: Cut 2 x GG, on the fold
Button loop: Cut 1 x X, on the bias

This versatile little bag is just the right size to carry your essential items, either during the day or for an evening out, and the buttons mean that you can easily adjust the length of the strap. I gave it a slightly more vintage and worn-in look by washing and tumble-drying, to soften up the new fabric.

The seam allowance throughout is 1cm

1 Zigzag the side and bottom edges of the front and back. Pin, then seam the two pieces together along these edges, with right sides facing.

2 Press the seam allowances open. Join the corners in a 't-junction' as shown on page 22 and neaten the seam allowance. Turn right side out.

3 Make up the button loop, following the rouleau instructions on page 25. Trim it to 8cm and stitch the ends together to form a loop. With raw edges matching and the loop facing downwards, stitch the ends of the rouleau to the centre top of the back, on the right side.

top tip → IF YOU DON'T FANCY MAKING BUTTONHOLES, SIMPLY DECIDE YOUR STRAP LENGTH, THEN SEW THE TWO ENDS DIRECTLY ONTO THE SIDES OF THE BAG. YOU CAN THEN ADD THE BUTTONS AS A DECORATIVE FEATURE.

Shoulder Bag

4 Join the side edges of the facings, with right sides together. Press the seams open and press under a 1cm allowance along the bottom edge.

5 Slip the facing over the top of the bag with right sides together. Line up the side seams, then pin and machine stitch around the top edge. Turn the bag wrong side out.

6 Turn the facing over to the wrong side of the bag and press around the top edge. Tack the bottom edge of the facing to the bag and stitch it down, 3mm from the fold.

7 Top stitch around the opening.

8 Pin tack and stitch the two strap pieces together with right sides facing, leaving an 8cm gap along one edge. Press the seam allowance back on each side of the gap. Notch the seam allowance at the curved ends, as shown on page 23.

9 Turn the strap right side out and ease out the curves. Slip stitch the gap. Press, then top stitch 3mm from the edge. Work two buttonholes at each end, either by hand or machine.

10 Sew one button to the centre front and one to each side seam, positioning them centrally between the two lines of stitching, then button the strap in place.

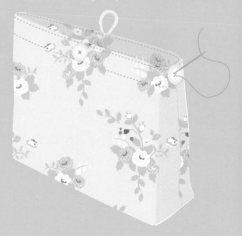

top tip → YOU COULD GIVE THE BAG A MORE STRUCTURED LOOK BY ADDING A LINING AND A SOLID BASE AS I DID FOR THE SHOPPER BAG VARIATION ON THE NEXT PAGES.

Shopper Bag

what you will need...

• 45 x 75cm floral print cotton duck • 35 x 75cm contrasting print for lining • 10 x 20cm rectangle of thick card • magnetic bag fastener or large press stud • 40cm 4cm-wide webbing • matching sewing thread • sewing kit • sewing machine

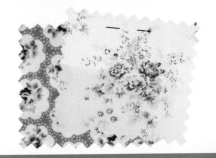

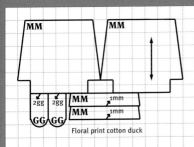

drawing up the pattern

Facing: Use piece MM with line 1mm as the bottom edge
Tab: Use piece GG with line 2gg as the straight edge

cutting out

Front and Back: Cut 2 x MM from floral print cotton duck
Facing: Cut 2 from floral print cotton duck
Tab: Cut 2 from floral print cotton duck
Lining: Cut 2 x MM from contrast print for lining

The shoulder bag on the previous pages turned out to be such a useful shape and size that I just had to come up with a variation! This rather more structured version has a solid base, a contrasting lining and a shorter, fixed handle made from cotton webbing.

The seam allowance throughout is 1cm

1 Make up the bag and lining as for the first two steps of the shoulder bag, but don't turn the lining right side out. Place the cardboard at the bottom of the main bag, then slip the lining inside, matching up the side seams.

2 Attach the projecting part of the fastener to the curved end of one tab, on the right side, and 2.5cm up from the end. Tack the second tab on top with right sides facing.

3 Machine stitch around the long and curved edges of the tabs, leaving a 6mm seam allowance. Clip around the curve (see page 23) and turn right side out. Press lightly, avoiding the fastener, and top stitch the seam.

4 Pin the straight end of the tab to the centre top edge of bag, on the right side, with raw edges matching.

YOU WILL NEED TO SEW THROUGH SEVERAL LAYERS OF THICKER FABRIC, PLUS THE COTTON WEBBING, FOR THIS PROJECT. TO MAKE SURE THAT THE STITCHES REMAIN EVEN YOU SHOULD FIT AN EXTRA STRONG NEEDLE TO YOUR SEWING MACHINE.

Shopper Bag

5 Pin the webbing centrally to the sides of the bag, so that 3cm at each end projects above the top edge.

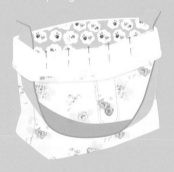

6 Make up and sew on the facing as in steps 4 to 6 of the shoulder bag. Work a rectangle of reinforcing stitches across each side seam, as shown on page 26.

7 Fix the recessed part of the fastener to the centre front of the bag, 5cm down from the opening.

8 Finish off the handle by pinning the two edges of the webbing together for 20cm along the centre. Stitch 3mm from the edge.

AS AN ALTERNATIVE TO COTTON WEBBING, YOU COULD MAKE THE HANDLE FROM AN 8 X 40CM STRIP OF MATCHING OR CONTRASTING FABRIC. PRESS THE STRIP IN HALF LENGTHWAYS, THEN PRESS UNDER A 1CM TURNING AT EACH LONG EDGE. REFOLD, TACK THE TWO LAYERS TOGETHER AND TOP STITCH 4MM FROM EACH EDGE.

Large Tote

what you will need...

- 65 x 140cm floral print cotton duck • 55 x 85cm spotted cotton
- stranded embroidery thread • button • matching sewing thread
- sewing kit • sewing machine

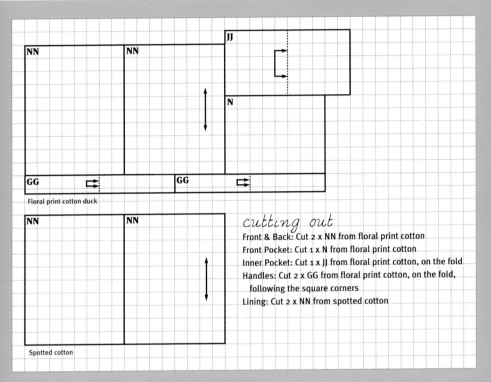

Floral print cotton duck

Spotted cotton

cutting out

Front & Back: Cut 2 x NN from floral print cotton
Front Pocket: Cut 1 x N from floral print cotton
Inner Pocket: Cut 1 x JJ from floral print cotton, on the fold
Handles: Cut 2 x GG from floral print cotton, on the fold,
   following the square corners
Lining: Cut 2 x NN from spotted cotton

This practical tote features my absolute favourite fabric pairing of large-scale roses and spots. It has a useful outside pocket and is roomy enough to carry books and files, or even a laptop, but it would also make a stylish and eco-conscious alternative to plastic carriers when you're out shopping.

The seam allowance throughout is 1cm

1 Press under 1cm, then a further 3cm along the top of the front pocket, then top stitch both folds. Make a buttonhole in the centre of the hem.

top tip

I MADE THE TOTE AND LINING FROM COTTON DUCK, WHICH MAKES IT VERY DURABLE, BUT YOU COULD LEAVE OUT THE LINING AND THE INNER POCKET TO MAKE A LIGHTER WEIGHT SHOPPING BAG THAT CAN BE FOLDED UP AND CARRIED IN YOUR HANDBAG.

Large Tote

2 Pin and stitch the pocket to the front bag piece, with raw edges matching. Pin the back of the bag to the front, with right sides together. Machine stitch side and bottom edges. Press under a 1cm, then a 4cm turning around the opening.

3 With right sides facing, sew the side and bottom edges of the two lining pieces together. Press the seam allowances inwards. Trim 5cm off the top edge.

4 Stitch a double hem along one short edge of the inner pocket. With right sides facing, fold in half widthways so the hem lies 5cm from the other short edge. Pin and seam. Trim the corners, turn right side out and press.

5 Mark a vertical line 7cm in from the right edge and machine to divide the pocket. Turn under the unstitched seam allowance at the top corners and slip stitch it down.

6 Pin the top edge of the pocket to the top of the lining, centring it on the back edge. Slip the lining inside the bag and fold the turning over to conceal the raw edges.

7 Make up the handles, neatening the short ends, as shown on page 27. Pin and tack the ends of one handle to the inside back of the bag, so that the edges line up with the pocket. Tack the other handle in the corresponding position on the front.

8 Work a round of stitching 6mm down from the top edge, then a second round, 3cm from the top edge. Work reinforcing stitching over the ends of the handles, as shown on page 26.

9 Finish off by sewing the button to the front of the bag, directly behind the buttonhole.

top tip

YOU CAN ADJUST THE STITCH LINE ON THE INNER POCKET SO THAT YOU HAVE A PERFECT FIT FOR YOUR PHONE AND PURSE, OR MAYBE ADD A NARROW CHANNEL FOR A PEN OR PENCIL.

Inside-out
Tote

what you will need...

- 75 x 140cm floral print cotton duck • 15 x 65cm spotted cotton
- 60cm 2.5cm wide webbing • 2m bias binding (optional)
- matching sewing thread • sewing kit • sewing machine

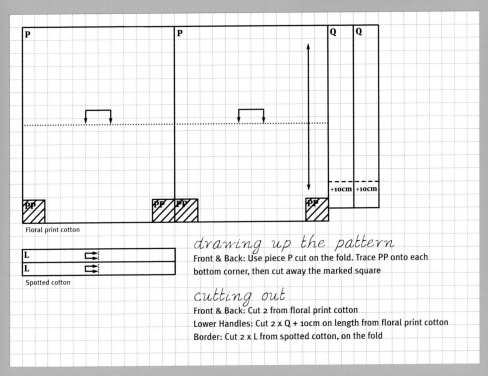

Floral print cotton

| L | ⇨ |
| L | ⇨ |

Spotted cotton

drawing up the pattern

Front & Back: Use piece P cut on the fold. Trace PP onto each bottom corner, then cut away the marked square

cutting out

Front & Back: Cut 2 from floral print cotton
Lower Handles: Cut 2 x Q + 10cm on length from floral print cotton
Border: Cut 2 x L from spotted cotton, on the fold

This ingenious folding bag is designed with two sets of handles, one in the usual place at the top, and a second pair positioned half-way down the sides. Fold the upper half of the bag to the inside if you just need the standard shopper shown opposite, or open it out completely for bulk purchases – see overleaf!

The seam allowance throughout is 1cm

1 Fold and press a turning 30cm down from the top edge of the front and back pieces to mark the positions for the lower handles.

2 Make up the two lower handles as shown on page 27, then trim each one to 65cm.

top
tip

I BOUND THE INSIDE SEAMS WITH BIAS TAPE TO GIVE THEM EXTRA STRENGTH, BUT YOU COULD ALSO FINISH THEM WITH A ZIGZAG OR OVERLOCKED STITCH SO THAT THEY WILL NOT FRAY.

Inside-out Tote

3 Position one handle across the front of the bag so that the top edge lies along the crease. Pin the two ends to the side edges of the bag then pin down a 22cm length at the left and right, leaving a 21cm unattached length in the centre.

4 Mark a 3cm rectangle at each end of the unstitched part. Top stitch the top and bottom edges of the pinned parts of the handle and work reinforcing stitching (see page 26) within the rectangles. Do the same on the back of the bag.

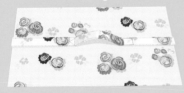

5 With right sides facing, pin and stitch the front and back together along the side and bottom edges, leaving the cut out corners free. Bind or overlock the seam allowances.

6 Join the corners with a t-junction seam, as explained on page 22. Fold one seam allowance to the left and one to the right at the point where the two lines of stitching meet, so that you do not have a bulky join.

7 Pin and stitch the ends of the two border strips together, with right sides facing. Press the seams open and press a 1cm turning around one edge.

8 Matching the seams, pin the border around the top edge of the bag, so that the right side faces the wrong side of the bag and the raw edges are aligned.

9 Cut the webbing in half to make two 30cm handles. Measure a point 22cm in from each top corner. Slip the ends of the handles under the border at these points: the ends should project above the top edge for 2cm. Tack the handles securely in place.

10 Turn the bag right side out and fold the border over. Tack down the folded edge, then top stitch both this and the top edge. Work rectangular reinforcing stitches over each end of the handle.

top tip

WHEN THE BAG WAS COMPLETE, I ONCE AGAIN DID MY SPECIAL TRICK OF WASHING IT ON A HOT CYCLE AND THEN TUMBLING UNTIL DRY, TO CREATE A SOFTER, MORE RELAXED APPEARANCE.

Quilted
Purse

what you will need...

• 55 x 35cm floral print cotton duck • 55 x 35cm cotton batting
• 55 x 35cm plain cotton • 35cm ricrac • large button • matching
stranded embroidery thread • pencil and clear ruler • matching
sewing thread • contrasting sewing thread for quilting • sewing kit
• sewing machine

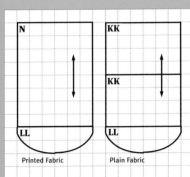

cutting out

Front & Back: Cut 1 x N from floral print cotton duck
Flap: Cut 1 x LL from floral print cotton duck
Bag lining: Cut 2 x KK following the square corners
Flap lining: Cut 1 x LL from plain cotton

The appeal of this project lies in the combination of carefully thought out details: the scalloped edge of the yellow ricrac insertion; the lines of pink quilting stitches; the hand-stitched buttonhole loop and the subtle gleam of a pearl button.

The seam allowance throughout is 6mm

1 Using a ruler and pencil, mark the quilting lines on the main bag and the flap by ruling a diagonal grid of 2.5cm squares on the right side of each piece.

2 Trim 6mm from each side of the flap pattern, then cut a piece of batting to this size. Tack the batting centrally to the wrong side of the flap and quilt the marked lines.

3 Tack a length of ricrac around the flap, so that the edge of the braid lies along the curved edge. Pin the flap lining to the right side of the flap.

4 Machine stitch along the curved edge. Clip the seam allowance (see page 23) and turn right side out. Ease out the curves and press lightly.

top tip IF YOUR FABRIC HAS AN OBVIOUSLY DIRECTIONAL DESIGN, CUT THE FRONT AND BACK PIECE WITH THE DESIGN RUNNING LENGTHWAYS. MAKE SURE THAT YOU SEW THE FLAP ONTO THE CORRECT END, OR THE PATTERN WILL APPEAR UPSIDE DOWN ON THE FRONT OF THE BAG.

Quilted Purse

5 Quilt the front and back piece of the bag as for the flap. With right sides facing, pin and stitch the straight edge of the flap to the top back edge of the bag.

6 Fold the bag in half lengthways with right sides facing and tuck the flap inside. Pin and stitch the side seams.

7 Stitch the two bag lining pieces together along the side edges. Press the seam allowances inwards, then press in a 1cm turning along the bottom edges. Turn right side out.

8 Slip the lining inside the bag so the right sides are facing and the seams aligned. Pin the top edges together so that the flap is sandwiched between the two. Machine stitch all around the opening.

9 Turn the bag right sides out through the opening and ease it into shape. Close the gap in the lining with slip stitch.

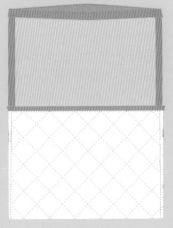

10 Work a buttonhole loop at the edge of the flap and sew the button to the front of the bag, in line with the loop.

top tip

I CHOSE A CLASSIC GRID PATTERN FOR THE HAND-QUILTING, THE SAME AS I USED ON THE HOTTIE. YOU COULD VARY THE STITCH PATTERN, DEPENDING ON YOUR FABRIC. IF YOU'RE WORKING WITH STRIPED FABRIC, FOR EXAMPLE, TRY QUILTING ALONG THE PARALLEL LINES.

T-Junction
Washbag

what you will need...

• 30 x 80cm floral print cotton • 30 x 65cm waterproof shower curtain fabric • 40cm nylon zip • 70cm bias binding • 10 x 20cm medium weight iron-on interfacing • matching sewing thread • sewing kit • sewing machine

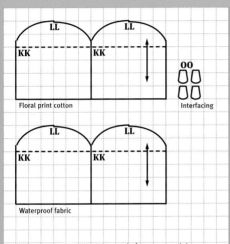

Floral print cotton

Interfacing

Waterproof fabric

drawing up the pattern

Side: Use piece KK, tracing around the entire outline and following the square corners. Add flap LL to the top edge.

cutting out

Bag: Cut two sides from floral print cotton
Lining: Cut two sides from waterproof fabric
Tabs: Cut 4 x OO from interfacing

I have always enjoyed finding new and unexpected uses for old fabrics, and this zip-up washbag started its life as a fifties sundress with a flouncy skirt! The wide turquoise and white stripes of the soft cotton are just perfect for the structured shape, which is finished off at the corners with t-junction seams.

1 Tack the lining pieces to the wrong side of the bag pieces, around all four edges.

2 Open out the zip and pin one straight edge along one curved edge of the bag, with right sides together. The zip is longer than the bag, so leave an equal overlap at each end.

3 Fit a zip foot to the machine and stitch down, 5mm from the teeth. Do the same at the other side. Press the seams outwards and top stitch, close to the stitch lines.

4 With right sides facing, pin and stitch the side and bottom edges together through all four layers. Leave 1cm unstitched at each top corner.

5 Join the bottom corners with a 't-junction seam' as shown on page 22. Turn right side out and slip the ends of the zip through the gaps at the top of the side seams. Slip stitch to close. Trim and bind the inside seams.

6 Iron the tabs onto the remaining fabric and cut out, leaving a 6mm margin all round. Tack this to the back, then slip stitch the tabs together in pairs, around the side and bottom edges. Trim the ends of the zip to 2cm and ease them through the top of the tabs. Stitch in place.

top tip

IF, LIKE ME, YOU CHOOSE STRIPES, YOU WILL NEED TO ALLOW A LITTLE EXTRA FABRIC SO THAT EVERYTHING MATCHES. MAKE SURE THE DESIGN LINES UP ON FRONT AND BACK, AND CUT FOUR IDENTICAL TABS WITH THE STRIPES RUNNING HORIZONTALLY.

Drawstring
Washbag

what you will need...

• 60 x 80cm patterned cotton • 35 x 45cm waterproof fabric • 70cm fine piping
cord • 70cm contrast bias binding • 70cm white bias binding • matching sewing
thread • ruler • sewing kit • sewing machine

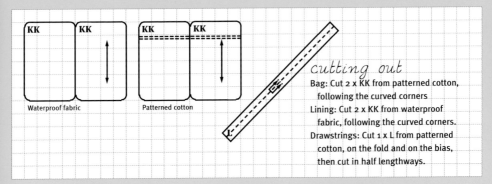

cutting out

Bag: Cut 2 x KK from patterned cotton,
following the curved corners

Lining: Cut 2 x KK from waterproof
fabric, following the curved corners.

Drawstrings: Cut 1 x L from patterned
cotton, on the fold and on the bias,
then cut in half lengthways.

Here's another quirky recycled dress fabric
– this time a painterly Sixties pattern of
brightly coloured squares. I found a length
of bias tape that proved to be the perfect
match for the vivid green and used this to
bind the main seam. The drawstring cords
are made from two long rouleaux, cut from
the main fabric.

1 Mark two points on each side, 6 and 7cm
down from the top edge of one bag piece.
Using a fading pen, rule between both sets
of points, so that you have two parallel
lines across the right side.

2 Pin the top part of the bag piece to a
lining piece, with right sides facing. Leaving
a 1cm allowance, machine stitch around the
top edge between the upper two points,
reinforcing both ends of the stitching.

3 Make a 1cm snip into both layers of
fabric, at the ends of the lower line. Clip the
corners, press the seam allowances inwards
and turn right side out.

4 Machine stitch along both lines to make
the drawstring channel, then make up the
second side in the same way.

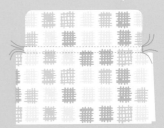

top tip

THIS PROJECT INTRODUCES YOU TO PIPED SEAMS AND ROULEAUX TIES – TWO
SLIGHTLY MORE ADVANCED TECHNIQUES THAT ARE MUCH USED IN DRESSMAKING
AND SOFT FURNISHINGS. DON'T BE PUT OFF HOWEVER, AS THE BAG IS NOT NEARLY
AS TRICKY AS IT MAY LOOK AT FIRST!

Drawstring Washbag

5 Cover the piping cord with the contrast bias binding, as shown on page 23. With raw edges matching and an overlap of about 3cm at each end, pin the piping to the right side of one bag piece. Fold the loose cord outwards at an angle.

6 Tack the second side to the first, with right sides facing.

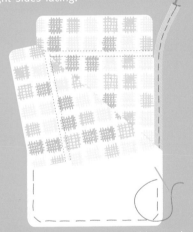

7 Fit the zip foot to your machine and sew the two sides together, close to the edge of the cord. Stitch over the angled ends of the piping. Trim the piping and clip the corners.

8 Neaten the seam allowance by covering it with the white bias binding, then turn right side out and press lightly.

9 Make up the two drawstrings as shown on page 25. Fasten a small safety pin to the first one and pass it through the gap between the two lines of stitching and along the drawstring channels on the front and back of the bag. Thread the second rouleau from the other side. Knot the ends of both cords and trim.

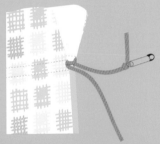

top tip

THE DRAWSTRINGS ARE MADE FROM VERY NARROW TUBES OF FABRIC. IF YOUR CHOSEN MATERIAL IS TOO THICK YOU WILL NOT BE ABLE TO DRAW IT THROUGH TO MAKE THE ROULEAUX, SO LOOK OUT FOR A FINE MATCHING COTTON INSTEAD. YOU COULD ALSO USE THIS FOR THE PIPING.

Jewellery Roll

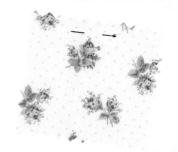

what you will need...

- 25 x 80cm floral print cotton duck • 20cm nylon zip • 1.5m bias binding
- 1 medium press stud • 50cm fine piping cord • matching sewing thread
- sewing kit • sewing machine

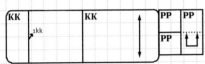

Floral print cotton duck

drawing up the pattern

Inside: Use piece KK, following the curved corners at the
left edge. Cut along line 1kk so you have two pieces.
Outside: Use piece KK, following the square corners at
the right edge. Trim 4cm from the left edge.

cutting out

Inside: Cut both parts from main fabric
Outside: Cut 1 from main fabric
Pockets: Cut 2 x PP from main fabric
Ring Holder: Cut 1 x PP from main fabric, on the fold

Keep all your bracelets, necklaces and brooches safe when you're out and about, by tucking them into the various compartments of this practical jewellery holder, then slide your rings onto the fabric tube. This project would make a great gift for all ages. It is perfect to take travelling or keep your precious jewels tucked away in a drawer.

1 Press under a 2cm turning along the right edge of the narrow inside piece and the left edge of the wide piece. Sew the zip between these folded edges (see page 25) and trim the projecting ends.

2 Stitch a narrow hem along one edge of each pocket and press a 6mm turning under the other three edges. With the hems on the left, pin them both to the right hand side of the inside piece, 2cm from the edges. Machine stitch down, close to the folds. Close the zip.

3 Press a 1cm turning along one long edge of the ring holder. Starting at the opposite edge, roll it up tightly with the right side outwards. Pin, then stitch down the fold. Neaten one end, with the seam at the back. Sew the projecting part of the press stud across the seam, 1cm up from the bottom edge.

top tip

IF YOU WANT TO MAKE A MORE PADDED JEWELLERY ROLL YOU COULD SANDWICH A LAYER
OF COTTON OR POLYESTER WADDING BETWEEN THE INSIDE AND OUTSIDE PIECES.

Jewellery Roll

4 Flatten out the open end of the ring holder. Pin, then stitch it securely to the top edge of the inside piece, 7cm to the right of the zip. Sew the second part of the press stud to the lower edge of the inside, in line with the first part.

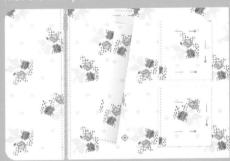

5 Pin the outside piece to the completed inside with wrong sides facing and trim to the same width. Machine stitch 6mm from the outer edge. Trim the seam allowance back to 3mm.

6 Using a fading pen, rule a line across the inside, 1cm to the right of the ring holder. Machine stitch along this line.

7 Starting at the centre left, neaten the outside edge with bias binding, stitching it down by hand or machine. Ease the folded edges round the curved corners, stretching it gently. Turn the binding under at a 45 degree angle at the square corners.

8 For the tie, cover the piping cord with the rest of the bias binding. Press under 1cm at one end, then wrap the binding over the cord. Slip stitch the folded edges together, neatening the other end in the same way. Fold the tie in half to find the centre and stitch this point securely to the centre left edge.

top tip

MAKE THE ROLL FROM A SMALL SCALE PRINT, SUCH AS THIS PRETTY ROSEBUD DESIGN, AND PICK OUT ONE OF THE DARKER COLOURS FOR THE BIAS BINDING AND TIES. INSTEAD OF USING THE SAME FABRIC ON BOTH THE INSIDE AND OUTSIDE, YOU COULD MAKE A PLAIN OR SPOTTED LINING.

Specs
Case

• 35 x 25cm floral print cotton duck • 35 x 50cm velvet • 25 x 35cm cotton batting • 75cm fine piping cord • small button • matching sewing thread • matching stranded embroidery cotton • sewing kit • sewing machine

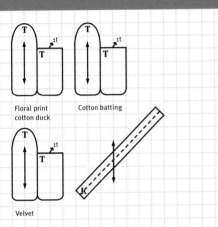

Floral print cotton duck

Cotton batting

Velvet

drawing up the pattern

Front: Use piece T, with line 1t as the top edge and following the curved corners

cutting out

Back: Cut 1 x T from floral print cotton duck, following the curved corners

Front: Cut 1 from floral print cotton duck

Back Lining: Cut 1 x T from velvet

Front Lining: Cut 1 front from velvet

Piping: Cut 1 x K from velvet, on the bias, then cut in half lengthways

Batting: Cut one front and one back

A round of vibrant pink piping gives a new twist to this classic spectacle case, and shows how you can transform an everyday item into something really individual by changing just one small design element. The case has a soft velvet lining and an inner padded layer to protect your specs or sunglasses.

1 Join the two bias strips, as shown on page 21 and use it to cover the piping cord (see page 23). Matching the raw edges, tack the piping around the outside edge of the back piece, starting at the centre bottom edge. Cross the two ends over where they meet, and trim the overlap.

top tip

THE VELVET PIPING HAS A GRAPHIC QUALITY, WHICH EMPHASISES THE OUTLINE OF THE CASE. THE BRIGHT PINK VELVET REALLY MAKES IT STAND OUT AGAINST THE GENTLE DOVE GREY BACKGROUND, SO PICK A STRONG COLOUR FROM YOUR MAIN FABRIC TO ACHIEVE THE SAME EFFECT.

Specs Case

2 Press a 1cm turning along the top edge of the front piece. With right sides facing, pin and tack the front to the back around the side and bottom edges. Fit a zip foot and stitch together. Trim the seam allowance to 6mm, clip the corners and turn right side out.

3 Trim away a margin of 1cm all around the outside edges of the front and back pattern pieces and use these as a guide to cut the batting. Tack the back batting centrally to the wrong side of the back lining, so there is a 1cm allowance all round.

4 Press a 1cm turning along the top edge of the front lining. Pin the batting to the wrong side, leaving a 1cm allowance all round. Fold the turning over the batting and tack.

5 With right sides together, pin, tack and machine stitch the front and back lining pieces together, leaving a 1cm seam allowance.

6 Trim the seam allowance on the side and bottom edges of the lining to 4mm.

7 Fold the surplus lining around the flap to the back of the batting, pleating it a little as you go around the curve, and tack it down.

8 Slip the finished lining inside the case, so the wrong sides are together. Ease the corners of the lining into place.

9 Slip stitch the top straight edge of the front to the top of the lining. Tack the flap lining back on to the flap and slip stitch it down around the curved edge, next to the piping.

10 Work a buttonhole stitch loop at the centre edge of the flap as shown on page 25. Sew a button to the front of the completed case, in line with the loop.

top tip

THE HANDMADE BUTTONHOLE LOOP, IN THE SAME GREY AS THE MAIN FABRIC, IS A WONDERFUL FINISHING TOUCH. IT IS NOT DIFFICULT TO DO, BUT IF YOU HAVEN'T USED THIS STITCH BEFORE, IT'S WORTH TAKING TIME TO PRACTISE THE TECHNIQUE ON A PIECE OF SPARE FABRIC.

iPod® Case

what you will need...

- 20 x 40cm printed fabric • 25cm square brushed cotton
- 25cm square cotton batting • 30cm 4cm-bias tape • 30cm fine cord
- spring cord toggle • matching sewing thread • sewing kit

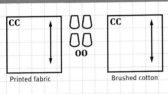

Printed fabric   Brushed cotton

cutting out

Bag: Cut 1 x CC from printed fabric
Tabs: Cut 4 x OO from printed fabric
Lining: Cut 1 x CC from brushed cotton
Padding: Cut 1 x CC from cotton batting

Traditional sewing techniques and the newest technology come together in this sweet little padded bag – the perfect safe home for your mobile phone or MP3 player. The drawstring fastening is made from nylon cord and secured with a spring toggle, which you can find at any good haberdashers.

1 Fold the bag in half with right sides facing. Pin, then seam the side and bottom edges together, leaving a 1cm allowance.

2 Press open the top 6cm of the side seam. Press a 2.5cm turning around the top edge, then turn the bag right side out.

3 Press a 2.5cm turning at each end of the bias tape, then press it in half lengthways with the turnings on the inside.

4 Tack the tape around the bag opening, with raw edges on the inside and 6mm of the folded edge projecting above the top edge. Line the folded ends of the tape up with the side seam.

5 Pin the lining to the padding and make up as in step 1. Press the seam allowances inwards, then press a 2.5cm turning around the top edge. Slip the lining inside the bag, positioning it so that the side seam is opposite the opening.

6 Tack the top edge of the lining to the top edge of the bag, stitching through the tape. Slip stitch the edges together.

7 Fasten a safety pin to one end of the cord and thread it through the tape channel. Slip two ends through the toggle.

8 Press under a 1cm turning along each tab piece, straightening off the curve at the bottom edges. Pin together in pairs and slip stitch the side and bottom edges. Push the ends of the cord through the openings and close with slip stitch.

I WAS LUCKY ENOUGH TO COME ACROSS A BINDING TAPE IN EXACTLY THE SAME SHADE OF ORANGE AS THE DETAILS ON THE DAISY PETALS, BUT IF YOU CAN'T FIND THE COLOUR YOU'RE LOOKING FOR, YOU CAN SIMPLY CUT A 4CM-WIDE BIAS STRIP FROM PLAIN FABRIC.

Addresses

Haberdasheries and fabric shops

All the Fun of the Fair
Unit 2.8
Kingly Court
Carnaby Street
London
W1B 5PW
020 7287 2303
www.allthefunofthefair.biz

Bedecked
5 Castle Street
Hay-on-Wye
HR3 5DF
01497 822769
www.bedecked.co.uk

Creative Quilting
32 Bridge Road
East Molesey
KT8 9HA
020 8941 7075
www.creativequilting.co.uk

Harts of Hertford
14 Bull Plain
Hertford
SG14 1DT
01992 558106
www.hartsofhertford.com

John Lewis
Oxford Street
London
W1A 1EX
and branches nationwide
08456 049049
www.johnlewis.com

Mandors
134 Renfrew Street
Glasgow
G3 6ST
0141 332 7716
www.mandors.co.uk

MacCulloch & Wallis
25–26 Dering Street
London
W1S 1AT
020 7629 0311
www.macculloch-wallis.co.uk

Millie Moon
20 Paul Street
Frome
Somerset
BA11 1DT
01373 464650
www.milliemoonshop.co.uk

Peabees Patchwork Bazaar
1 Hare Street
Sheerness
Kent
ME12 1AH
01795 669963
www.peabees.com

Rags
19 Chapel Walk
Crowngate Shopping Centre
Worcester
WR1 3LD
01905 612330

Sew and So's
14 Upper Olland Street
Bungay
Suffolk
NR35 1BG
01986 896147
www.sewandsos.co.uk

Tikki
293 Sandycombe Road
Kew
Surrey
TW9 3LU
020 8948 8462
www.tikkilondon.com

Sewing Classes

**Alison Victoria School
of Sewing**
71 Market Street
Ashby de la Zouch
Leicestershire LE65 1AH
www.schoolofsewing.co.uk

Liberty Sewing School
Regent Street
London W1B 5AH
www.liberty.co.uk

**Modern Approach Sewing
School**
Astra Business Centre
Roman Way
Ribbleton
Preston PR2 5AP
01772 498862
www.sewjanetmoville.co.uk

Sue Hazell Sewing Tuition
Southcombe House
Chipping Norton
Oxfordshire OX7 5QH
www.sewing-tuition.co.uk

The Studio London
Studio 5
Trinity Buoy Wharf
64 Orchard Place
London E14 0JW
www.thestudiolondon.co.uk

Fairs

**Great Northern Contemporary
Craft Fair**
Spinningfields
Manchester
www.greatnorthernevents.co.uk

Knitting and Stitching Show
Alexandra Palace
London and
RDS
Dublin and
Harrogate International Centre
01473 320407
www.twistedthread.com

Sewing for Pleasure
NEC
Birmingham
www.ichf.co.uk

A few handy websites:

DMC
www.dmccreative.co.uk
Sewing and embroidery threads.

Donna Flower
www.donnaflower.com
Online store of both antique
and vintage fabrics.

Etsy
www.etsy.com
An online marketplace for
everything handmade and
vintage, including fabric and
other sewing supplies.

Fabric Rehab
www.fabricrehab.co.uk
For vintage and contemporary
prints.

Ribbon Moon
www.ribbonmoon.co.uk
For ricrac and bias binding in a
wide range of colours and
widths.

So Vintage Patterns
www.sovintagepatterns.com
For a collection of over 4,000
vintage sewing patterns.

Vintage Fabric Market
www.vintagefabricmarket.co.uk
For antique fabrics, accessories
and other collectables.

Addresses

Cath Kidston's shops

Bath
3 Broad Street
Milsom Place
Bath
BA1 5LJ
01225 331 006

Battersea
142 Northcote Road
Battersea
London
SW11 6RD
020 7228 6571

Brighton
31a & 32 East Street
Brighton
BN1 1HL
01273 227 420

Bristol
79 Park Street
Clifton
Bristol
BS1 5PF
0117 930 4722

Chelsea
12 Cale Street
London
SW3 3QU
020 7584 3232

Cheltenham
21 The Promenade
Cheltenham
GL50 1LE
01242 245 912

Chiswick
125 Chiswick High Road
London
W4 2ED
020 8995 8052

Covent Garden
28–32 Shelton Street
London
WC2H 9JE
020 7836 4803

Dublin
Unit CSD 1.3
Dundrum Shopping Centre
Dublin 16
01 296 4430

Edinburgh
58 George Street
Edinburgh
EH2 2LR
0131 220 1509

Fulham
668 Fulham Road
London
SW6 5RX
020 7731 6531

Guildford
14–18 Chertsey Street
Guildford
GU1 4HD
01483 564798

Harrogate
4–6 James Street
Harrogate
HG1 1RF
01423 531481

Heathrow Airport
Departure Lounge
Heathrow Airport
TW6 3XA
020 8759 5578